A COMPENDIUM OF
— CURIOUS —
COLORADO PLACE NAMES

JIM FLYNN

THE
History
PRESS

Published by The History Press
Charleston, SC
www.historypress.net

Copyright © 2016 by Jim Flynn
All rights reserved

Front cover image of Bishop's Castle courtesy of Wikimedia Commons.

First published 2016

Manufactured in the United States

ISBN 978.1.46713.732.4

Library of Congress Control Number: 2016947528

This book is dedicated to my parents, who taught me to respect the past and challenge the future. May they rest in peace.

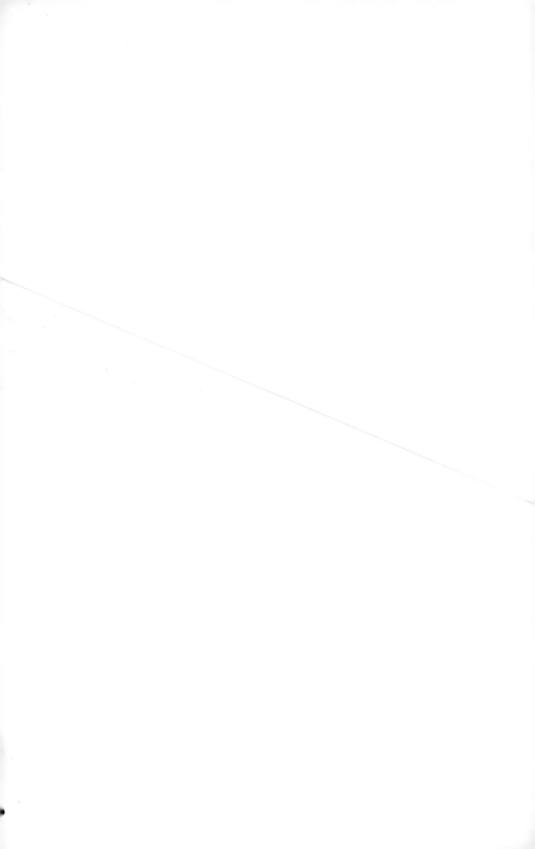

CONTENTS

Preface

As I was driving into the Colorado high country not long ago in pursuit of late season/hungry/throw-caution-to-the-wind trout, it occurred to me that although I had lived in this beautiful state more than forty years, I knew very little about the origin of its place names. I decided it was time to remedy that situation, and I began tracking down information about these names.

I quickly discovered that every name came with a story, and those stories were interesting and entertaining. Taken together, they told much of the history of Colorado. I also quickly discovered I wasn't the only longtime Colorado resident (to say nothing of visitors to our state) who knew little about this state's place names and where they came from. By way of example, in the course of writing this book, after many inquiries, I never found anyone who knew how Denver got its name. Additionally, Siri, although polite and apologetic, was of only occasional help.

Initially, my thought was to put the information I had gathered into something like a travel guide—just an alphabetical list of names with a snippet of name origin information attached to each. But the good folks at The History Press, the publisher of this book, had a better idea—organize the material into chapters grouping names together that had a common source of inspiration, like Native Americans, explorers, geologic and geographic landmarks and so on, and include brief background material for each of these organizational categories. So, that's what I have done. (If you're looking for a particular name, the index at the end of the book will take you there.)

You won't, of course, find all Colorado names here. There are too many. I've focused on names that have piqued my curiosity like, say, Slumgullion, or that come with an unusual story attached like, say, Breckenridge. Most names with an obvious derivation—eagle, beaver, coyote, Washington, Lincoln, Kennedy, Reagan, Harvard, Yale, Democrat, Republican, Elway, Manning, Helton and so on—have largely been excluded.

I also need to add that this book is not, for the most part, a work of original scholarship. Rather, I have relied on information gathered by others, and some of what you find here may be as much legend as fact. But the legends, if that's what they are, are intriguing.

I would be remiss in not recognizing the digging and sifting accomplishments of others who have worked diligently to uncover the origin of Colorado place names, notably George R. Eichler and his successor, William Bright, who carried on Eichler's scholarship after his death (*Colorado Place Names*, third edition, Johnson Books, Boulder), as well as Maxine Benson, who added to the list of names addressed by Eichler and Bright and sometimes found competing theories of name origin (*1001 Colorado Place Names*, University Press of Kansas). I'm also indebted to Carl Abbott, Steven J. Leonard and Thomas J. Noel, authors of *Colorado: A History of the Centennial State*, fifth edition (University Press of Colorado). This book helped me understand what was happening in Colorado during the times most of the place names referenced in my book were being created.

If you find a name that isn't in this book and you think it should be (and you know where the name came from), let me know and I'll include it in the next edition.

INTRODUCTION

As you would expect, Colorado place names come from a multitude of sources. This includes the Spanish empire and its North American successor, Mexico, and their fondness for saints and other religious references. It includes Native Americans, who can trace their roots back many thousands of years to the days of wooly mammoths and primitive tools and who had most of Colorado to themselves until the 1800s. But then the great European-American western migration began, and Native American populations were decimated by warfare, white man's diseases, shrinking animal herds due to overhunting and, some would argue, genocide.

Also in the mix of place name originators are the explorers who endured incredible hardship and danger to explore and map what is now Colorado and to climb its highest mountains on their day off. (All of this took place before REI and Gore-Tex.) North American mountain men are part of this group, although their objective was not so much to explore and map as it was to kill beavers and send their pelts back to Europe, where beaver hats were held in high esteem as a men's fashion item. If it hadn't been for a change in European fashion preference from beaver hats to silk hats, the beaver population in Colorado might have been exterminated. These poor critters—busy building dams, lodges and ponds and paying no attention to their safety—didn't seem to realize that they were on their way to regional extinction. Soldiers also belong in this group since their military assignments often included exploration. In addition, a substantial military presence was necessary in Colorado during its formative years to support the western

European-American migration, and a substantial military presence has continued ever since, now to protect against (or be prepared to engage in) space and cyber warfare.

Then we have the prospectors, lured to Colorado by an 1859 gold rush, a silver boom in the 1870s, another gold rush in the 1890s and a realization that coal and other mineral deposits in Colorado could be exploited for profit. Although Colorado was—and continues to be—famous for refining the concept of boom and bust, prospectors and miners were the most prolific at this enterprise. After the 1859 gold rush flamed out, there were as many people trudging across the Great American Desert from west to east as there were from east to west.

Next we have the railroads. Despite the immense capital needed to build a rail line, there were dozens of railroad companies trying to lay tracks and gain shipping monopolies throughout the Colorado Territory (and, starting in 1876, the state of Colorado). Most went broke, but a few survived. The competition was fierce, including at one point armed conflict between two railroad companies vying to establish a rail line from Pueblo to Leadville along the Arkansas River. Until the arrival of rail service, reaching Colorado from take-off points along the Missouri River corridor required a miserable multi-day/multi-week stagecoach or ox cart trip across the prairies. In addition to wholly uncomfortable transportation devices (shock absorber technology was in its infancy), travelers had to endure blizzards, dust storms, rain, hail, tornados, rattlesnakes, swarming insects, bandits and hostile Indians if they wanted to get to Colorado. Railroads changed all that and made the journey to Colorado almost pleasant (probably more so than today's air travel). The railroads established new towns along their routes and gave them names, with the names, in most cases, lasting far longer than the railroads.

As a regular source of place names, we also have politicians, entrepreneurs and promoters, many of whom overlapped. They saw the potential for income enhancement that Colorado had to offer and were willing to take huge risks and exaggerate to others (to the point of outright fraud) the chances for entrepreneurial success in pursuit of personal gain. Fortunes were made and often lost again. But along the way, these individuals built infrastructure, created a system of laws and the means to enforce them and established a (mostly) democratic form of government that allowed the state, albeit in fits and starts, to grow and prosper. Many Colorado places were named after these players to honor their accomplishments (and feed their egos).

Agriculturalists—farmers and ranchers—were also responsible for many Colorado place names. These were often ordinary (and sometimes desperate) folks, including many immigrants, who packed up their belongings and came to Colorado to try their hand at farming and ranching in the arid West, in pursuit of a better life for themselves and their families. (In some cases, they came for the gold and stayed for the sugar beets.) However, there were also large amounts of agriculture-related capital imported into Colorado when times were good and the fruit hung low. Many farmers and ranchers failed, some held on by their fingertips but survived and some (in particular those who learned how to use free resources provided by the federal government) accomplished great things and achieved significant wealth.

In this category, we also have other pioneers and settlers who may have given agriculture a try and, when that didn't work out, moved on to other activities in pursuit of an income. Some people came to Colorado with the intent to carry on with an existing profession or occupation, thinking there might be a better market out west for their skills. These pioneers and settlers, in addition to the agriculturalists, were often responsible for naming a town or other location where they found themselves.

As part of the naming of places in Colorado by transplants to the area, the United States Post Office, predecessor to our current United States Postal Service, played an important role. That's because a goal of every new community was to obtain an official U.S. Post Office designation, and the postal service had the final say on the names assigned to the new post offices it approved. U.S. Post Office officials in charge of name assignments were apparently not selected based on spelling skills, and this resulted in frequent name mutations that have nonetheless survived.

Also on our list of inspirational sources for place names are geographic and geologic phenomena—for example, unusual rock formations—and flora and fauna. On the flora and fauna side of things, the result has been considerable duplication of effort. For example, Colorado has seventy-two Willow Creeks, forty-nine Bear Creeks and forty-eight Dry Creeks. It has forty-nine streams and a luxury ski resort named Beaver Creek, and there are ten Beaver Lakes and four Beaver Mountains.

The last organizational category I have created is for the misfits. Although many place names referenced in this book could appropriately be placed into more than one category, there are a few that didn't seem to fit any of the categories. These are the misfits.

Since there are frequent references in this book to the counties of Colorado, I've started you off with a map showing the state's sixty-four counties. When Colorado first became a territory in 1861, there were only seventeen counties. But after that, there was a regular, and often contentious, shuffling of county borders, resulting in gives and takes that produced the current configuration.

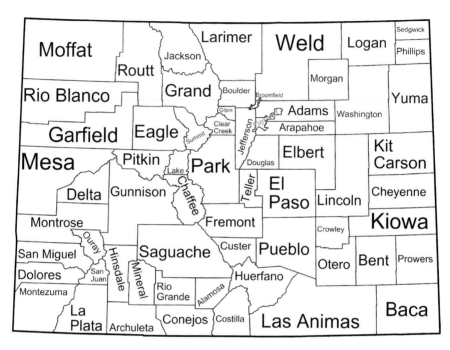

Colorado's sixty-four counties. There may be logic here, but it doesn't leap out at you. *David Benbennick via Wikimedia Commons.*

CHAPTER 1

THE SPANISH EMPIRE
AND ITS PROGENY

The Spanish empire, notwithstanding its collapse in the 1800s, had a great deal of influence on Colorado place names. Although trying to explain in a few paragraphs Spain's colonization efforts in North America is like trying to explain in a few paragraphs the origin of the universe, here is generally how it went.

The Spanish empire got going big time after Christopher Columbus's famous visit to the New World in 1492. Over the next century, Spain expanded its reach to the point where the sun never set on its areas of conquest and control.

From 1519 to 1521, through brutal warfare (and help from deadly European diseases), Spanish conquistador Hernán Cortés managed to wipe out the Aztec civilization in Central America and establish a substantial Spanish presence in what is now Mexico. Spanish colonization then began moving north. In 1540, Francisco Vasquez de Coronado, another of Spain's marquee conquistadores, led a 1,300-member expedition from central Mexico into New Mexico. Although Coronado's expedition didn't make it to what would eventually become Colorado, it came close.

In further pursuit of northward (and eastward) expansion, in 1598, Juan de Oñate, a Spanish provincial governor, led an expedition of five hundred men and soldiers into northern New Mexico and established a settlement there. A half century later, Juan de Archuleta took an expedition from that location into Colorado.

Spain, however, what with trying to control the entire world and all, didn't have the resources to maintain a firm grip on its most northerly North American territories. In 1680, a bloody Indian revolt chased Spanish settlers and military personnel out of the area. Between 1692 and 1696, Spain managed to reconquer New Mexico, but Indian raids on Spanish settlements continued, creating a notable deterrent to civilian relocation. The Indians, it seems, were introduced to horses by the Spanish, and not too long after that, they became masters at using horses to disrupt Spanish attempts at colonization in New Mexico and Colorado.

Spain then ran into another problem. In the late 1600s and early 1700s, French traders and settlers from St. Louis and Louisiana began working their way west into what is now southeastern Colorado and northeastern New Mexico. The French found it productive to create alliances with various Indian tribes and used those alliances to restrict Spanish influence in the area. This activity peaked in the mid-1700s.

However, in 1763 and as a consequence of other world events, France ceded its claim to land in the North American heartland to Spain. This turned on the green lights for a man named Juan Bautista de Anza to lead a large expedition from New Mexico into Colorado. Anza was the governor of New Mexico, having been given that position in appreciation for his helping Spain establish San Francisco as an important port and settlement. Anza's objective on his expedition was to shut down disruptive Comanche Indians, and his travels took him north across the Rio Grande, along the west side of the Sangre de Cristo Range, around the north side of Pikes Peak and into what is now Manitou Springs and Colorado Springs. But any attempt by the Spanish to colonize this area fizzled when Napoleon, in 1800, took back the land France had previously given to Spain. Three years after that, the United States acquired this land as part of the Louisiana Purchase, which included much of Colorado.

In the early 1800s and notwithstanding Napoleon's meddling and the Louisiana Purchase, Spain still laid claim to a substantial part of Colorado. In 1819, when the United States and Spain couldn't agree on the location of the line separating their respective territories, they, in order to avoid warfare (or worse, litigation), entered into a treaty known as the Adams-Onis Treaty. This treaty left intact Spain's claim to a sizeable chunk of Colorado.

But the world continued to turn, and in 1821, Mexico achieved independence from Spain. After three hundred years or so of colonialism, Spain was gone, and the Mexican revolutionary government, ragged though it was, found itself in control of much of what is now the Southwest

United States, including the land in Colorado assigned to Spain in the Adams-Onis Treaty.

Then, in 1846, the United States and Mexico got crosswise over the ownership of Texas, which had been annexed into the United States as a new state in 1845. This led to the Mexican-American War. To the extent anyone actually wins wars, the United States came out on top in this affair, and as part of the 1848 Treaty of Guadalupe Hidalgo, the United States acquired most of Mexico's claim to what are now the southwestern states, including Colorado. Finally, in 1853, the United States purchased some additional land from Mexico, which became a part of the south end of Arizona and New Mexico.

To round out the picture of Colorado's territorial evolution, in 1850, Texas—now a state after its 1845 annexation into the United States—gave up some of its land as part of a complex politically brokered rearrangement of state and territorial borders called the Compromise of 1850. This deal was driven by the issue of slavery—that is, which states would be slave states and which would not. Texas wanted to be a slave state, and it had to agree to give up some of its land to achieve that objective. A part of the land relinquished by Texas ended up being included in the Colorado Territory when it was formed in 1861, as well as a part of the state of Colorado when it was formed in 1876.

In brief summary of this dash through Spain in North America history, as of 1848 and the Treaty of Guadalupe Hidalgo, the United States finally had ownership of all of what is now Colorado. However, the legacy of the Spanish empire—as a matter of language, religion, agricultural practices, art, architecture, music, food, drink, law and, yes, place names—has lived on.

ACASCOSA. This name (pronounced ah-kahs-*kos*-uh) is likely a mutation of the Spanish words *agua ascosa*, meaning stagnant water. A lake, at 10,984 feet in south-central Colorado (Conejos County), has this name. The lake is sometimes referred to by another unflattering name: Bog Lake.

ALAMEDA. *Alameda* is a Spanish word meaning something like "cottonwood grove" and has frequently been used as a name for streets, schools, light-rail stations and so on in and around Denver and other parts of the state.

Alamosa. *Alamosa* is another Spanish word that, in one way or another, refers to groves of cottonwood trees. And there are lots of these in Colorado, especially along the banks of the Rio Grande as it crosses through the San Luis Valley in south-central Colorado, where the city and the county of Alamosa are located. The name Alamosa was given to the city by the Denver and Rio Grande Railway when it established a major operation there in 1878. Alamosa County came into being quite a bit later, in 1913. The San Luis Valley is an important agricultural area, rich in history going back long before Colorado was first visited by people of European descent. The Great Sand Dunes National Park and Preserve is partly in Alamosa County. As an oh-by-the-way, the other national parks in Colorado are Rocky Mountain, Mesa Verde and Black Canyon of the Gunnison River.

Animas. The Animas River, which runs through Durango on its way to a downstream confluence with the San Juan River, was given the name *Río de las Ánimas*—River of the Souls—a long time ago by a Spanish explorer. Which one, however, is a matter of controversy. It was possibly Juan María de Rivera, who was wandering around this part of the world in 1765 at the request of the governor of what was then New Mexico. Or it might have been the Franciscan monks Dominguez and Escalante, who passed through the area in the 1770s while on their (unsuccessful) search for a land route from the Spanish mission in Santa Fe to the Spanish missions in central California. The name morphed into just the Animas River at some later time, and that's now the river's official name.

Antonito. *Antonito* means "Little Anthony" in Spanish and derives from the Spanish name for Saint Anthony: *San Antonio*. In south-central Colorado (Conejos County), we have the San Antonio River and the San Antonio Mountains. Those names, in turn, led to the Antonito name being given to a town along the Conejos River, founded in 1881 by the Denver and Rio Grande Railway. As for Saint Anthony, well, he was an early day monk from Egypt who gained fame by going off into the wilderness by himself to reinforce his Christian faith. While he was there, he was confronted with a barrage of supernatural temptations (some involving seductive women), all of which he was apparently able to resist. This not only got him sainted but has also inspired multiple paintings depicting the "temptation of Saint Anthony," including works by Salvador Dalí, Max Ernst and Hieronymous Bosch. (If you're not familiar with Bosch, he was an early Netherlands painter who lived from 1450 to 1516 and created some of the weirdest paintings ever made. He was essentially the first surrealist, although that name wouldn't be invented until the early twentieth century. Bosch's paintings make Salvador Dalí look like a landscape artist.)

BLANCA. *Blanca* is the feminine iteration of the Spanish word for "white." Blanca Peak, a part of the Sangre de Cristo Range, towers over the San Luis Valley, which lies some 7,000 feet below the summit. At 14,345 feet, Blanca Peak is Colorado's fifth-highest mountain. The small town of Blanca, named after the mountain, is in Costilla County along Colorado Highway 160 at the southern base of the mountain and at the west end of North La Veta Pass.

CEBOLLA. *Cebolla* (pronounced seh-*boy*-uh) is the Spanish word for onion. Cebolla Creek has its headwaters near Slumgullion Pass and flows northward all the way to Blue Mesa Reservoir. There are wild onions growing in the valley through which the creek runs, the likely inspiration for its name. There are trout in Cebolla Creek, but they are wary critters that (in my experience) have a knack for knowing the difference between real food and imitations thereof offered by fishermen.

CERRO. *Cerro* (pronounced *sair*-oh) is the Spanish word for "hill," and someone lacking imagination used this word to name a high point along U.S. Highway 50 east of Montrose and west of Gunnison. Cerro Summit tops out at 8,042 feet, high enough to make winter driving there exciting. In the summer, you need to look out for large herds of sheep using U.S. Highway 50 as a shortcut to new pasturage. If you encounter such an event, watching the dogs at work moving the sheep along makes the delay in your travels worthwhile.

CHICO. In the Spanish language as spoken in Colorado and New Mexico, *chico* (pronounced *chee*-ko) is the name given to a shrub-like desert plant frequently found in the Southwest, including parts of Colorado. It has edible berries, which were a part of the diet of some Indian tribes who were perhaps tired of eating buffalo (or could no longer find buffalo because European-American hunters had killed them all). Chico Creek is a small tributary of the Arkansas River, with its headwaters in El Paso County. After a fifty-four-mile journey, it enters the Arkansas just upstream from the town of Avondale, in Pueblo County.

Cimarron. This name comes from the Spanish word *cimarrón*, which means "wild, unruly," making it an appropriate name for all manner of places in Colorado (and many children). The Cimarron River, in Montrose and Gunnison Counties, is a significant tributary of the Gunnison River, joining the Gunnison upstream from the Black Canyon of the Gunnison River National Park. This river is not to be confused with a larger and longer multi-state Cimarron River that begins in northeast New Mexico and briefly crosses through Colorado in its far southeast corner on its way to a confluence with the Arkansas River in Oklahoma. There is also a small town along U.S. Highway 50, east of Montrose and next to the smaller river, named Cimarron.

Colorado. *Colorado* is the Spanish word for "ruddy," referring to a reddish brown color. Early Spanish explorers gave this name to the Colorado River (*Rio Colorado*), which in some places carries a great deal of silt and has this color. The name was then given to the Colorado Territory when it was formed in 1861 out of parts of the territories of Kansas, Nebraska, New Mexico and Utah. The name carried over to the state of Colorado when it was established in 1876, earning it the right to call itself the Centennial State. The land that is now Colorado was assembled by the United States through the Louisiana Purchase (1803); a war with Mexico, which resulted in Mexico ceding land to the United States (1848); the annexation of the Republic of Texas (1845); and a deal cut with the State of Texas in 1850. (Some Colorado residents are of the opinion that based on the occasional questionable behavior of tourists from Texas, this annexation should never have been allowed to occur and the Republic of Texas should have remained a separate country.)

Conejos. *Conejo* is the Spanish word for "rabbit," and *Conejos* (pronounced kuh-*nay*-hos) would seem to be the Spanish word for more than one rabbit. Conejos County, bordering New Mexico in south-central Colorado, was created in 1861 as one of the original seventeen counties that made up the Colorado Territory. The county gave up a significant amount of its original land to other Colorado counties in 1874 and again in 1885. The county was originally named Guadalupe County, but that name was soon changed to Conejos in recognition, presumably, of the large number of rabbits living in the area.

CORTEZ. This name comes from Hernán Cortés de Monroy y Pizzaro (just Hernán to his friends). He lived from 1485 to 1547 and was one of the conquistadors given the task of colonizing the New World for the glory of Spain. Cortés gets credit for conquering Mexico and wiping out the Aztec empire. The town of Cortez, in far southwest Colorado not far from the Four Corners, was founded in 1886 as a place to house men working on a water diversion project intended to take water out of the Dolores River and send it to the Montezuma Valley for irrigation. As a small bit of irony, Cortez is the county seat for Montezuma County, named, like the valley, after the Aztec chief who lost his job (and his life) thanks to the exploits of Hernán Cortés.

COSTILLA. *Costilla* (pronounced kos-*tee*-uh) is a Spanish word for "rib," which most likely explains why a tributary of the Rio Grande that begins in New Mexico and joins the Rio Grande in Colorado is named the Costilla River. This river, in turn, served as inspiration for the name given to Costilla County, one of the original seventeen counties that made up the Colorado Territory when it was formed in 1861. The county lost land to neighboring counties in 1866, 1874 and 1913. The oldest town in Colorado, San Luis, is in Costilla County. That town was incorporated by Hispanic settlers from Taos, New Mexico, in 1851. The oldest continuously operating Colorado family business, the R&R Market, is located in San Luis. The R&R, as it's called by the locals, first opened its doors in 1857. Prior to the naming of Costilla County, Colorado had a town named Costilla. However, in 1925, a long-standing boundary dispute between Colorado and New Mexico, which went all the way to the U.S. Supreme Court for decision, caused this town to end up in New Mexico.

CRESTONE. This name comes from the Spanish word *crestón*, which can be variously translated as "top of a cock's comb," "crest of a helmet" or, if you're into prospecting, "outcropping of ore." Crestone Peak and Crestone Needle are two of Colorado's fifty-three "fourteeners"—mountains topping 14,000 feet in elevation. Crestone Peak, at 14,294 feet, ranks seventh on the list. Crestone Needle, at 14,197 feet, ranks nineteenth. The two Crestone-named mountains are in the Sangre de Cristo Range and involve two of the more dangerous Colorado fourteener ascents. The small town of Crestone, at the east end of the San Luis Valley, has developed a reputation as a hangout for people into New Age spiritualism (and as a possible landing site for space aliens when they finally visit Earth).

CUCHARAS. *Cucharas* (pronounced koo-*char*-us) is the Spanish word for "spoons." In Colorado, the Cucharas River, a seventy-five-mile tributary of the Huerfano River with its headwaters south and west of the Spanish Peaks, took its name from the spoon-shaped valley through which it flows. This, in turn, led to the naming of a pass connecting Huerfano and Las Animas Counties, again in south-central Colorado. Cucharas Pass, sometimes shown on maps as Cuchara Pass (only one spoon), tops out at 9,938 feet and is crossed by paved Colorado Highway 12. The town of Cuchara is along Highway 12 on the north side of the pass. Highway 12 has been given the nickname the "Highway of Legends Scenic Byway" and is one of several highways in Colorado having a scenic and historic byway designation.

CULEBRA. *Culebra* (pronounced kuh-*lee*-bruh locally) is the Spanish word for "snake." So, various things in Colorado that are snakelike in shape carry this name. (For many years, I lived on a winding street in Colorado Springs named Culebra Avenue.) Culebra Peak is the southernmost of Colorado's fourteeners, occupying, at 14,047 feet, position number forty-one on the fourteeners list. The name for this mountain was already established by the early 1800s and may have come from previously named Culebra Creek, which has a snakelike course. In any event, there's nothing about the mountain that resembles a snake. Culebra Peak is unique among Colorado's fourteeners in that it is privately owned. If you want to climb Culebra Peak, you need to make a reservation and pay a fee—$150 per person as of this writing.

CUMBRES. *Cumbres* is a Spanish word meaning "summits," and the name was given to a pass, among other places, in southwest Colorado. A railroad line was first built over this pass in the earlier 1880s by the Denver and Rio Grande Railway. The line connected Alamosa on the east with Durango on the west. Today, only the Cumbres and Toltec Scenic Railroad uses the rail line, for tourist excursions during the tourist season. The tourist train begins and ends its journey at Antonito. Colorado Highway 17, a paved road, also crosses over Cumbres Pass. The summit of the pass is at 10,022 feet. Assuming you don't count the high point on Trail Ridge Road as a pass (most people don't because it's flat), Cumbres Pass comes in thirty-eighth on the list of Colorado passes crossed by an improved road. (The name Toltec, by the way, refers to an Indian civilization that existed in central Mexico from the tenth through the twelfth century, before there were trains.)

DEL NORTE. *Del norte* means "of the north" in Spanish, and the early Spanish name for what is now the Rio Grande was *Río Grande del Norte*—"Great River of the North." The town of Del Norte, which is located along the river and is the county seat for Rio Grande County, was given this name when the town was founded sometime around 1872.

DOLORES. This name made it into Colorado history thanks to an early Spanish explorer, Juan María Antonio Rivera. Rivera, in 1765, named a river he came upon, in what is now southwest Colorado, *Río de Nuestra Señora de los Dolores*, meaning "River of Our Lady of Sorrows." Since remembering the full name for this river proved challenging, the river came to be known simply as the Dolores River. The river, some 250 miles long, is a tributary of the mighty (at least until it gets to Mexico) Colorado River. One of Colorado's sixty-four counties, in the southwest corner of the state, was given the Dolores name in 1881. Archaeological studies have shown that this part of Colorado was inhabited as early as 2500 BC and had a thriving population of something like ten thousand between AD 900 and 1300, after which drought or disease or other events beyond their control (absence of a good shopping mall?) caused these people to relocate. Canyons of the Ancients National Monument, administered by the Bureau of Land Management, is in Dolores County. Just to the south, in Montezuma County, is Mesa Verde National Park, famous for the Anasazi cliff dwelling ruins located there. The small town of Dolores, Colorado, sits along the Dolores River, at the upper end of McPhee Reservoir, some forty miles from the Four Corners Monument.

DURANGO. This name, given to a city in southwest Colorado along the Animas River, comes from Durango, Mexico, which in turn took its name from Durango, Spain, which in turn took its name from a word in the Basque language (*urango*) meaning something like "water town." Durango, now the county seat in La Plata County, was formed in 1881 by the Denver and Rio Grande Railway after the town of Animas City, a few miles to the north, refused to grant the railroad the concessions it had demanded as a condition to establishing a depot there. This was shortsighted on the part of the citizens of Animas City, since it no longer exists and Durango has prospered.

EL PASO. One meaning of *el paso* in Spanish is "the passage," and this was the Spanish name given to what later came to be called (and is still called) Ute Pass, a route around the north side of Pikes Peak that gold rushers used to reach the mining fields surrounding Cripple Creek and Victor when, in the early 1890s, the second Colorado gold rush moved in that direction. El Paso County was named for this pass. It was one of the original seventeen Colorado counties established when Colorado became a territory in 1861. In 1899, a chunk of El Paso County on its west side was carved off and made a part of newly formed Teller County. El Paso County is the most populous county in Colorado, since the sprawl around Denver covers multiple counties. El Paso County's most famous landmark is Pikes Peak, the easternmost mountain in Colorado—and the United States—with an elevation above 14,000 feet (14,110 to be exact). Pikes Peak was formerly known as Pike's Peak, but after years of heated debate among grammatologists, the apostrophe was dropped. This change has not received universal acceptance and is still a source of occasional grumbling.

HUERFANO. *Huérfano* (pronounced *wear*-fan-oh) means "orphan" in Spanish. The name was given to a dark mound of volcanic rock—Huerfano Butte—that sits all by itself in an otherwise mostly flat area just to the east

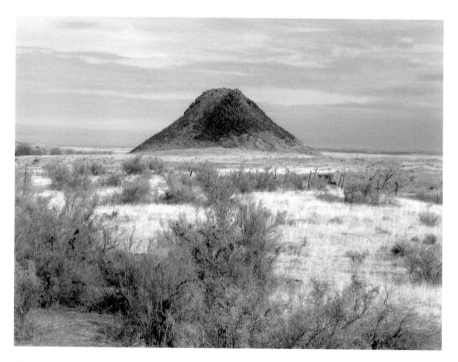

Huerfano Butte—the orphan. A longtime traveler's landmark in what is now south-central Colorado, just north of Walsenburg. *NordNordWest via Wikimedia Commons.*

of Interstate 25 and north a few miles from Walsenburg, in south-central Colorado. The name was then given to one of Colorado's original seventeen counties, created at the time Colorado became a territory in 1861. When first formed, Huerfano County took up most of the southeast corner of the Colorado Territory. Then, however, it went through several geographic shufflings, giving up land to Las Animas County and Pueblo County, as well as a county called Greenwood that only lasted four years before it became Bent County and Elbert County. In yet another shuffling, Huerfano County finally got land back from Fremont County.

LA GARITA. This is a Spanish word meaning "lookout," and the name (pronounced la gar-*ee*-tuh) was given to a 13,710-foot peak in south-central Colorado (Saguache County) where, legend has it, Indians would generate smoke signals that could be downloaded to the east, across the San Luis Valley, in the Sangre de Cristo Range. (Smoke signals may still be a more reliable form of communication in this remote area than cellphones.) The La Garita name was then given, in the 1870s, to a small town east of the peak, a creek and a 129,626-acre wilderness area.

LA JARA. In the Spanish language, at least as spoken in Colorado and New Mexico, *la jara* (pronounced la *har*-uh) is the name of a type of willow—the sandbar willow—that grows along the banks of rivers in southern Colorado and northern New Mexico. In Colorado, we have the small town of La Jara (population 818 as of 2010), La Jara Reservoir and La Jara Creek, all off the beaten path in south-central Conejos County, south and west of Alamosa.

LA JUNTA. *La junta* (pronounced la *hunt*-uh) means "the junction" in Spanish. This was an appropriate name for a new town founded around 1875 along the rail line of the Kansas Pacific and Santa Fe Railroad as it passed through the plains of southeast Colorado. That's because the town site was where the Santa Fe Trail crossed the Arkansas River. For several decades before the railroads arrived, the Santa Fe Trail was a major commercial highway between Independence, Missouri, and Santa Fe, New Mexico. On the theory that this was, after all, their land, the Comanche Indians tried for a while to charge tolls for use of the Santa Fe Trail. However, this restraint on interstate commerce didn't sit well with west-moving settlers, so the Indians were regularly attacked and eventually chased out of the area. La Junta, now a city, is the county seat for Otero County.

La Manga. *La manga* means "the sleeve" in Spanish, and someone decided long ago that this would be a good name for a mountain pass that, after all, is much like a sleeve through the mountains. So, we have La Manga Pass in southwest Colorado. This pass lies between better-known Wolf Creek Pass to the north and the New Mexico border to the south. It rises to 10,250 feet and is traversed by a paved road, Colorado Highway 17, which begins in Antonito on the east and ends at the New Mexico border on the west. (This road also takes you over Cumbres Pass.) In light of La Manga Pass's proximity to Wolf Creek Pass, which receives more snow than any other part of Colorado and where it can snow any time of year, having a reliable weather and road report in hand before heading over the pass is always a good idea.

La Plata. *La plata* (pronounced la *plah*-tuh) means "the silver" in Spanish. In southwest Colorado, you'll find the La Plata River, the La Plata Mountains and La Plata County. The county was formed in 1874 out of land originally part of Lake County and Conejos County. La Plata Peak is Colorado's fifth-highest mountain, located in the Sawatch Range in the west-central part of the state. It tops out at 14,336 feet.

Las Animas. This name comes from the Spanish name given long ago to the river in south-central Colorado now known as the Purgatoire River. The original name for this river was *El Rio de las Ánimas Perdidas en Purgatorio*, which translates in English to the "River of the Lost Souls in Purgatory." Since no one could ever fully remember this, the name of the river got shortened to Purgatoire, and the name of a Colorado county got shortened to Las Animas. Las Animas County was formed in 1866 as a carve-out from Huerfano County. Although sparsely populated, Las Animas County is the largest (in land mass) of Colorado's sixty-four counties.

Mancos. *Mancos* is the plural of a Spanish word meaning something like "one-handed," "faulty," "crippled," "maimed" or "imperfect." So, how did this name come to be associated with a small town (which calls itself the Gateway to Mesa Verde) and a river in far southwestern Colorado? Well, the town was apparently named after the river. As for the river, reference to the Mancos River shows up as early as 1776 in the journals of Franciscan monks Dominguez and Escalante, created during their unsuccessful journey in search of an overland route from the Spanish mission in Santa Fe to Spanish missions in California. One account of the use of the name Mancos traces its origin to an earlier New Mexican Spanish monk, Father Salvero, who was injured in an accident involving the river while exploring in the area with his Indian guide, Juan. The accident, the story goes, resulted in the amputation of one of Father Salvero's legs, crippling him and leading to the naming of the river. Another account ties the name to the crippled condition of the horses of a group of early Spanish explorers following an arduous crossing of the San Juan Mountains.

MANZANOLA. This name seems to be a play on the Spanish word for apple, *manzana*, or apple tree, *manzano*. The name was given to a town along U.S. Highway 50 in eastern Colorado (Otero County) that had plentiful nearby apple orchards. The town dates back to 1869 and was originally known as Catlin. The Manzanola name was adopted in 1900, presumably to highlight and promote the apple growing industry in the area.

MEDANO. *Médano* is the Spanish word for "dune" or "sand dune." Medano Pass (9,931 feet) appropriately gets its name because the road across it either starts or finishes—depending on your direction of travel—in what is now the Great Sand Dunes National Park and Preserve, in Alamosa County, on the west side of the Sangre de Cristo Range. On the other side of the pass, to the east, is Westcliffe, Colorado, in Custer County. The road over the pass requires a 4x4 vehicle with a driver indifferent to scratched paint and willing to ford several streams (not recommended during spring runoff). Zebulon Pike's expedition crossed the pass on January 27, 1807. Pike described this in his journal as "a bad day's march." He probably could have picked a better time of year.

MOLAS. We have a lake and a mountain pass in the San Juan Mountains in southwestern Colorado bearing this name, but its derivation is uncertain. One theory is that the name refers to the mole-like mammals common in this area and that someone who didn't speak Spanish very well thought *molas* was the Spanish word for moles, which it is not. Another theory is that the name resulted from a misspelling of the Spanish word for mules, *mulas*. In any event, Molas Pass is a mountain pass rising to 10,910 feet, traversed by U.S. Highway 550 and a part of the Million Dollar Highway connecting Ouray and Silverton. Along this road, the pass that gets most attention is Red Mountain Pass, which presents numerous opportunities for accidental death thanks to steep cliffs, an absence of guardrails, oversized RVs driven by flatlander tourists, avalanches and so on. Molas Pass is a walk in the park compared to Red Mountain Pass. The origin of the Million Dollar Highway name is also disputed. One theory is that it cost $1 million per mile to build the road back in the 1920s. Another theory is that its fill dirt contains $1 million in gold ore. Take your pick.

MONTEZUMA. This name comes from the famous Aztec king who ruled from 1502 to 1520. His real name was Moctezuma II, but somewhere along the way, this got recast as Montezuma. Montezuma was promptly killed during the Spanish conquest of Mexico by soldiers under the command of conquistador Hernán Cortés. It was once thought that the cliff dwelling ruins in southwestern Colorado, now preserved as Mesa Verde National Park, were of Aztec origin, and in 1889, before this theory was discredited, Montezuma County was named. Montezuma County is the most southwesterly county in the state and was formed out of land originally a part of La Plata County. This area was inhabited as early as AD 600 and may have had a population of 100,000 in the twelfth century, before global warming or some such thing caused everyone to relocate.

MOSCA. This name comes from a famous (or infamous) Spanish explorer and conquistador, Luis de Moscoso Alvarado. He lived from 1505 to 1551 and spent his time conquering places in Mexico and Central America, often with his even more famous uncle, Pedro de Alvarado. History has it that one of his scouting parties made it into the San Luis Valley and the Sangre de Cristo Range around 1542, to include passage over what is now known as Mosca Pass, named in his honor. This pass is a (relatively) low notch (9,737 feet) on the west side of the Sangre de Cristo Range immediately to the east of the Great Sand Dunes National Park and Preserve. The pass has played a role in the formation of the Great Sand Dunes since it attracts westerly flowing winds full of sand, but the sand is too heavy to go over the mountains and ends up being deposited in what is now the national park. An interpretive trail up to the summit of the pass starts in the park. There is also a town named Mosca, seventeen miles north of Alamosa and near the park. This town is the home of the Colorado Gators Reptile Park, an eighty-acre wetlands area fed by a geothermal well that hosts a population of alligators (not indigenous), other reptiles and birds. The park claims that some 120 species of birds have, at one time or another, stopped by for a visit.

NATURITA. This name, given to a creek and a small town in far west Colorado (Montrose County) first established in the 1880s, comes from a Spanish word meaning "little nature." The name was chosen by an early resident, Mrs. Rockwell Blake, to reflect the fact that the town, which sits along the San Juan River, is a lush oasis in comparison to the barren landscape that surrounds it.

PIEDRA. *Piedra* (pronounced pee-*ed*-ruh) is the Spanish word for "rock," so it gets lots of play in Colorado. Of particular note, the Piedra River is a significant tributary of the San Juan River. The Piedra River has its headwaters in the San Juan Range and then flows forty miles in a southwesterly direction before entering the San Juan River at the upper end of Navajo Lake.

PINOS. *Pinos* (pronounced *pee*-nohs—you need to be careful with this) is the Spanish word for "pine trees," so, like *piedra*, the Spanish word for "rock," it has been used frequently in Colorado to name things. Of particular note, there are at least four rivers and streams in Colorado that use the name *pinos*.

PLATORO. This name comes from a combination of the Spanish words for silver (*plata*) and gold (*oro*) and was given, in the 1870s, to a high country mining camp in what is now Conejos County. Both silver and gold were mined in this area. Platoro Dam, near the headwaters of the Conejos River, forms Platoro Reservoir, which has a surface area of 1.5 square miles and a storage capacity of fifty-three thousand acre feet. If you want a get-away-from-it-all vacation, this may be your place. Platoro Reservoir claims to be the highest man-made lake in North America, and there is no cellphone service in the area.

PONCHA. There is only speculation about where this name (pronounced *pon*-chuh) came from. It might have derived from a Ute Indian word or a Spanish word (as spoken in New Mexico) relating to tobacco or a tobacco-like plant. It might also have come from some other Spanish word, such as *poncho*, which, among other things, means "lazy." In any event, the name was given long ago to a fairly gentle (lazy...) pass in south-central Colorado, between the Sangre de Cristo Range on the east and the Sawatch Range on the west. Poncha Pass (9,010 feet) is crossed by Colorado Highway 285, with Alamosa to the south and Buena Vista to the north.

PUEBLO. *Pueblo* (pronounced *pweb*-lo by most people but pee-*eb*-lo by some of the locals) is a Spanish word meaning "village" or "people." A trading post called El Pueblo or Fort Pueblo was established along the Arkansas River in what is now the city of Pueblo in 1842. But it was put out of business by a violent Indian attack in 1854. The settlement got going again in 1858 and 1859 when the Colorado gold rush hit its stride. The city of Pueblo, Colorado's third-largest municipality, was the result of a merger of four separate towns—Pueblo, South Pueblo, Central Pueblo and Bessemer. The first three came together in 1886. Bessemer was the last to join, in 1894. Pueblo County was formed in 1861 as one of the original seventeen counties making up the Colorado Territory. At one time, the city of Pueblo was known as the saddle making capital of the world. A devastating flood of the Arkansas River hit the city in 1921. Today, the river walk along the Arkansas River in downtown Pueblo is a wonderful community resource, and the upstream Pueblo Dam should protect the city from further devastating floods.

RATON. *Ratón* (pronounced rah-*tone*) is a Spanish word for "mouse" and, as used in Colorado and New Mexico, is also a word meaning "squirrel" or "ground squirrel." Raton Pass (7,834 feet) probably got its name because of the large population of these critters in the area. This pass has been used for centuries, providing the best connection between south-central Colorado and north-central New Mexico. Raton Pass was part of the original Santa Fe Trail, first laid out by Captain William Becknell in 1821. Today, Interstate 25 crosses over Raton Pass, and despite its southerly location and relatively modest elevation, the pass is not a place you want to be during a snowstorm. Giving it a certain western panache, several country/folk singers and songwriters have seen fit to mention Raton Pass in their repertoire, including Townes Van Zandt, C.W. McCall and Clint Black.

RICO. *Rico* (pronounced *ree*-koh) is the Spanish word for "rich," and some grizzled old miner chasing silver in the 1870s, after the Ute Indians had been forced out of the area, decided this would be a good name for a mining camp. The mining camp morphed into the small town of Rico in Dolores County, in far southwest Colorado. These days, the residents mine tourism rather than silver as their primary source of economic activity.

RIO BLANCO. *Río blanco* means "white river" in Spanish, and this was the name first given to a 195-mile river (now called the White River), which has its headwaters in northwest Colorado and flows in a southwesterly direction into Utah, where it empties into the Green River. The Rio Blanco name lives on thanks to a northwest Colorado county. Rio Blanco County was formed in 1889 out of land taken from Garfield County.

RIO GRANDE. *Río grande* means "big river" in Spanish, and the Rio Grande is indeed a big river. Its headwaters are in the rugged San Juan Mountains in southwest Colorado. The river goes south to South Fork and then heads east across the San Luis Valley, passing through Alamosa along the way. After that, it takes a hard right and flows into New Mexico. From there, the river eventually works its way to the Gulf of Mexico. By the time it reaches the Gulf, the river has shrunk a good bit due to irrigation depletions. The Rio Grande has an overall length of some 1,896 miles, although this measurement has to be adjusted from time to time due to naturally occurring changes in the riverbed. Rio Grande County, in south-central Colorado, was formed in 1874 out of land taken from Costilla County and Conejos County.

SALIDA. *Salida* (pronounced suh-*lie*-duh) is a Spanish word meaning "outlet" and was chosen as a town name because it's at this location that the Arkansas River makes a sharp turn to the left, widens a bit and heads off in an easterly direction. The town was founded in 1880 when the Denver and Rio Grande Railway made it to this spot. The railroad initially named the town South Arkansas, but that didn't catch on with the locals, who much preferred the soft and sensual-sounding name Salida. Alexander Hunt, then an executive with the railroad and later a governor of the Colorado Territory, and his wife are given credit for coming up with the name Salida.

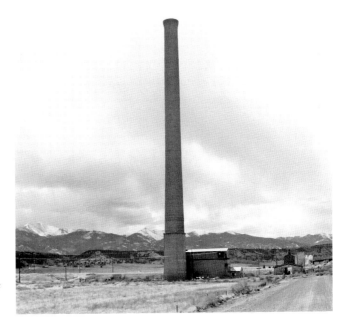

Smokestack of the Ohio-Colorado Smelting & Refining Company near Salida. It's 365 feet tall. For comparison, the Leaning Tower of Pisa is 179 feet, and the Washington Monument is 555 feet. Bad timing here: this facility began operations in November 1917, and by March 1920, it was already economically obsolete and was shut down. *Photo by author.*

SAN CRISTOBAL. This is the Spanish name for Saint Christopher and is the name given to Colorado's second-largest natural lake. Lake San Cristobal is in Hinsdale County, at 9,003 feet, near the town of Lake City, which was named for the lake. The lake was formed when a geologic phenomenon, the Slumgullion Earthflow, created a dam across the Lake Fork of the Gunnison River. Now, as for Saint Christopher, he was apparently a giant of a man— some seven and a half feet tall. He is the patron saint of travelers and earned that position by carrying people across a dangerous river they could not otherwise cross. Legend has it that one of his passengers, after a particularly difficult crossing of the river, revealed himself to Saint Christopher as Jesus Christ. This firmed up Saint Christopher's allegiance to Christianity, and when some heathen king later ordered him to make a sacrifice to a pagan god, he refused and was, well, beheaded.

SANGRE DE CRISTO. *Sangre de Cristo* is Spanish for "blood of Christ." How the name came to be assigned to the southernmost subrange of the Rocky Mountains is not known. One theory has it that the name derived from the dramatic red-colored sunrise and sunset alpenglow the Sangre de Cristo Range produces, especially in the winter. In all events, the name has been in use since at least the early 1800s, although the range has had other names, including, appropriately, the Snowies. These mountains are as steep, rugged and beautiful as anything Colorado has to offer.

SAN JUAN. We can thank Spanish influence and religious history for this name, which translates in English to Saint John. For those rusty on their religious history, Saint John is most famous for predicting the arrival of, and baptizing, Jesus. Colorado is home to the beautiful and rugged San Juan Mountains in the southwest part of the state, as well as the headwaters of the San Juan River. The San Juan River, some 383 miles in length, begins in the San Juan Mountains and then flows south and west through New Mexico and Utah, on its way to Lake Powell, where it joins the Colorado River. A chance to chase big rainbow trout in a tail water section of the river, below Navajo dam in northwest New Mexico, is on the bucket list of every fly fisherman ever born. San Juan County was formed in 1876—the year Colorado became a state—out of land taken from Lake County. San Juan County has the highest mean elevation, at 11,240 feet, of any county in the United States. And while we're at it, twenty-three of the top twenty-five highest mean elevation counties in the United States are in Colorado. New Mexico and Utah make the list with one county each.

SAN LUIS. *San Luis* (pronounced san-loo-*ees*) is the Spanish iteration of Saint Louis and comes to us from Louis IX (1214–1270), who became king of France in 1226 at the tender age of twelve. No doubt a record at the time, Louis IX held on to the throne without revolution or assassination until his death from natural causes, some forty-four years later, in 1270. Louis IX is the only French king to be canonized. (The rest of them have, for the most part, been demonized.) Places all over the world have been named after Saint Louis. Here in Colorado, the town of San Luis, in the south-central part of the state, is the state's oldest incorporated town, first established in 1851. It was a part of the New Mexico Territory until 1861, when the Colorado Territory was formed. The large fertile valley along the Rio Grande in south-central Colorado also carries the San Luis name, as does one of Colorado's 14,000-foot peaks. San Luis Peak, at 14,017 feet, ranks either forty-ninth or fiftieth on the list of Colorado's fifty-three fourteeners, in competition with nearby Wetterhorn Peak. (There is a mere 1-foot difference in the summit elevations of these two mountains, no matter whose list you look at.) San Luis Peak is located in the San Juan Range in southwest Colorado, a considerable distance from the town of San Luis.

SAN MIGUEL. *San Miguel*—Saint Michael—is another name given to Colorado places as a consequence of Spanish influence and religious history. Saint Michael is reported to have had a distinguished career as an archangel, is looked on as a chief opponent of Satan and is credited with saving souls at the hour of death. San Miguel County in southwest Colorado was formed in 1883 out of land taken from Ouray County. The county name came from the San Miguel River, which has its headwaters in the area and flows north and west for ninety miles until it joins up with the Dolores River, near the Colorado-Utah border. The river drops seven thousand feet in elevation from its headwaters to its junction with the Dolores River. Telluride, now in competition with Aspen as a hangout for wealthy skiers, is the county seat of San Miguel County.

TRINCHERA. *Trinchera* is a Spanish word meaning "trench." The name was given long ago to a creek in south-central Colorado because the creek forms something of a trench through what is otherwise a prairie. In addition to the creek, there is a small town in Las Animas County named Trinchera, and Trinchera Peak (13,517 feet) is in neighboring Costilla County. We also have the Trinchera Ranch, totaling some 171,400 acres that, in 2007, was acquired by billionaire Louis Bacon, founder of a large hedge fund called

Moore Capital Management. Bacon bought the property from the five children of another rich guy, Malcom Forbes, for $175 million. This sale occurred after a conservation easement prohibiting development was placed on the property, reducing its value but generating a substantial tax deduction for its owners. The Trinchera Ranch is the largest remaining undeveloped tract of land within the boundaries of the historic Sangre de Cristo land grant. It has also been a generator of litigation of various sorts (most notably, claims to hunting and fishing rights by nearby residents) for decades, helping to feed the families of many lawyers.

Trinidad. This is a Spanish word associated with the Holy Trinity. However, how it came to be the name of a town (now a city) in south-central Colorado near the New Mexico border back in the 1860s is uncertain. One theory is that the name was merely intended to honor the Christian tradition of the Holy Trinity. But another theory has the name coming from a beautiful woman named Trinidad who caught the fancy of one of the men, Gabriel Gutiérrez, involved in naming the town. (Said woman was apparently not Gutiérrez's wife.) Trinidad has a rich and colorful history. Famous gunslinger Bat Masterson (1853–1921) was the town's marshal for a period of time in the 1800s (before he started making western movies for television). Trinidad also became known as the sex change capital of the world after a doctor specializing in sex reassignment surgery, Stanley Biber, set up shop there in the late 1960s.

Vallecito. This name comes from a Spanish word meaning "little valley" and has been used in Colorado for Vallecito Reservoir and the dam that forms it, Vallecito Dam. The dam impounds water from the Pine River. The primary purpose for constructing the reservoir was irrigation, but it has become an important recreation site as well. The reservoir is north and east of Durango and has a surface area of 4.3 square miles. There are many backcountry trails starting out at the reservoir and heading off into the rugged San Juan Mountains.

Vega. *Vega* is a Spanish word meaning "fertile plain," and as Spanish was spoken in the early days of what is now Colorado and New Mexico, the word referred to pastureland. Colorado has used the name for a state park in Mesa County. The highlight of the park is Vega Reservoir, a two-mile-long lake that sits in a high (eight-thousand-foot) meadow on the northeast edge of Grand Mesa National Forest.

VETA. *Veta* (pronounced *vee*-tuh) is the Spanish word for "seam," which is a logical name for a mountain pass. So, we have North La Veta Pass (9,413 feet), traversed by Colorado Highway 160, a main road going all the way from Walsenburg on the east to Cortez in far southwest Colorado (and additionally famous for its crossing of Wolf Creek Pass). We also have Old La Veta Pass (9,380 feet), which lies to the south a bit. Old La Veta Pass apparently worked fine as a rail route, but because of some tight curves, it didn't work as a motor vehicle route. Old La Veta Pass is now crossed by a seldom-used backcountry gravel road. To further complicate things, there is also Veta Pass (9,220 feet) to the south of Old La Veta Pass. As with Old La Veta Pass, this has been used as a rail route but not a motor vehicle route. North La Veta Pass is kind and gentle, and very scenic, during good weather. I can tell you from experience, however, that it's not a place you want to be in a blizzard. It was in the late 1980s, and I was traveling west to east across this pass with my son, heading home to Colorado Springs after a day of skiing at Wolf Creek. We found ourselves in a complete whiteout long before we reached the summit and survived only by following a semi-trailer truck over the pass. Although the truck driver seemed to know what he was doing and where he was, my son and I were never too sure whether we were on the highway or driving through a hay meadow.

CHAPTER 2

NATIVE AMERICANS

Since long before, and during, the great European-American westward migration, Colorado was home to (or at least a spring break destination for) multiple Native American tribes. This included the Apaches, the Navajos, the Utes, the Shoshones, the Comanches, the Cheyennes, the Pawnees, the Kiowas and the Lakota Sioux. In many cases—in particular with the Utes—these tribes were more in the nature of loose federations of independent bands rather than cohesive units of governance. Of common importance to the cultures of these tribes, however, were abundant game, fertile soil and, after Francisco Coronado's visit to New Mexico in 1540–42, horses.

The Indian tribes present in Colorado routinely fought, and formed alliances, with one another and with the foreign invaders coming into their territories from Spain, France and the United States. Overall, the story of the Indian populations in Colorado is a tragic one—a story of changing times and clashing cultures, filled with villains and heroes, diplomats and scoundrels, assassins and peacemakers.

In their confrontations with the foreign invaders, the Indians were sometimes the prevailing party—Little Big Horn, the Meeker Massacre and others. Most times, however, they were not—the Sand Creek Massacre, the Battle of Summit Springs and many more. In the end, the Indians most certainly were not the prevailing party, having been evicted from their native lands and herded onto reservations in parts of the country no one else much wanted (at least until the discovery of oil, gas and other valuable minerals on some of this land).

In all events, for our purposes, the legacy of the Native American populations in Colorado lives on in the form of many of this state's place names.

ACHONEE. This name (pronounced ah-*choh*-nee), given to a 12,649-foot mountain in the Indian Peaks Wilderness, comes from a Cheyenne Indian subchief named Ochanee, which means "one-eye" in the Cheyenne language. Ochanee was one of the many Indians killed when a 700-member unit of the Colorado Territorial Militia attacked a peaceful Cheyenne and Arapahoe Indian village in 1864 in what became known as the Sand Creek Massacre. Somewhere between 70 and 163 Indians were killed, and an estimated two-thirds of those were women and children. The soldiers mutilated the bodies of their victims and took body parts as trophies of their "victory."

AMACHE. This name comes from the daughter of Cherokee Indian subchief Ochanee ("one-eye" in the Cherokee language), who was killed during the 1864 Sand Creek Massacre. Amache, known to her friends and family as "Amy," married John Prowers the year before her father was killed. John Prowers was a well-known and well-respected early settler in southeast Colorado who came to be a wealthy cattleman and who served for a time in the Colorado legislature. Prowers County, in far southeast

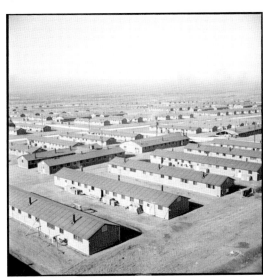

Granada Japanese American relocation center (aka Camp Amache), near Granada, Colorado. Not Colorado's finest hour. *Tom Parker, U.S. National Archives and Records Administration.*

Colorado, is named for him. Amache's name lives on in the form Camp Amache, officially called the Granada Relocation Center, where thousands of people of Japanese ancestry, many of them U.S. citizens, were incarcerated following the attack on Pearl Harbor. A museum telling part of the story of this sad event in U.S. and Colorado history can be found in the nearby Prowers County town of Granada.

Antero. This name comes from a chief of the Uintah band of Ute Indians. The name translates to "graceful walker." The Utes occupied land in what became Colorado for some six centuries before they were herded off to reservations in Utah, Colorado and New Mexico. Chief Antero is remembered as a proponent of peace with the white man (although history will forever debate whether this was the right path for his tribe to follow). Mount Antero, the eleventh-highest peak in Colorado at 14,269 feet—2 feet lower than number ten Grays Peak—is a spectacular mountain that rises some 7,000 feet above the floor of the Upper Arkansas River Valley between Buena Vista on the north and Salida on the south. It has deposits of aquamarine and other semi-precious stones that keep weekend prospectors busy in a search for enhanced wealth. Antero Reservoir is an on-again/off-again water storage facility along a part of the South Platte River in Park County that, when not drained due to drought conditions, stores water for the Denver metropolitan area and can grow some really big trout.

Apishapa. The Apishapa River, a tributary of the Arkansas River in south-central Colorado, got its name from an Indian word meaning (depending on whom you talk to) either "stinking water" or "mossy water." The river sometimes ceases to flow in the summer months and leaves stagnant pools that then become mossy and have an unpleasant smell. However, the Apishapa River Valley is, overall, a scenic agricultural area not far from the border between Colorado and New Mexico.

Arapahoe. This name, also spelled Arapaho, comes from one of the Indian tribes that was prominent in Colorado when the white man's great western migration began. The tribe apparently used another name for itself, but the Arapahoe name, coming from the language of another tribe, stuck. A peaceful village of the Arapahoe and Cherokee tribes got in the way of the Colorado Territorial Militia in 1864, giving rise to what became known as the Sand Creek Massacre. The name Arapahoe has been given to many places in Colorado, including a county that lies just east of Denver and is part of the Greater Denver metropolitan statistical area. Arapahoe County claims to be Colorado's first county since there was an Arapahoe County in existence as a part of the Kansas Territory before the Colorado Territory was formed. The discovery of gold in 1858 in what is now Arapahoe County started the Pikes Peak gold rush, although this discovery was a long way from Pikes Peak.

ARIKAREE. Arikaree is one of several names given to a tribe of Plains Indians who had a presence in Colorado when civilization came west and reprogrammed their culture. In September 1868, members of the Arikaree tribe, together with members of the Cheyenne and Arapaho tribes, were involved in one of the last major Indian/U.S. Army engagements in Colorado. The soldiers positioned themselves on an island in what is now known as the Arikaree River in Yuma County. That island was later named Beecher Island in honor of Lieutenant Frederick H. Beecher, who was killed in the fighting, and this confrontation became known as the Battle of Beecher Island. On a more positive note, one of the Indian Group mountains in Grand and Boulder Counties is named Arikaree Peak, with a summit elevation of 13,150 feet.

CHAMA. Colorado has a very old small town named Chama in the south-central part of the state (Costilla County), near the New Mexico border and not far from better-known Chama, New Mexico. Also, the Chama River, a tributary of the Rio Grande, which is mostly in New Mexico, has its headwaters in Colorado. The name is a derivation of a Tewa Indian word that, bizarrely, translates into something having to do with wrestling, such as "here we have wrestled" or "old wrestling village."

CHERAW. This name (pronounced cher-*awe*) comes from a place and an Indian tribe in South Carolina that somehow made its way west to Colorado as the name of a lake in Otero County, north and east a bit from Rocky Ford. A small town that grew up near the lake then took on the name of the lake. Cheraw, South Carolina, is in the northeast part of that state, not far from the North Carolina border, and has a population of some 5,800, considerably larger than Cheraw, Colorado, which had a population of 252 at the time of the 2010 census.

CHEYENNE. The Cheyenne Indians were one of several horse-culture Plains Indian tribes having a significant presence in Colorado. Many places in

Colorado carry the Cheyenne name, including a county in east-central Colorado. Things did not go well for the Cheyenne tribe when settlers pushed into Colorado in the 1800s. Numerous battles were fought between the Cheyennes and the U.S. Cavalry, mostly during the 1860s and 1870s, after the United States largely ignored treaties entered into with the tribe. Significant during this period was the Sand Creek Massacre—November 29, 1864—where a 700-man unit of the Colorado Territorial Militia attacked a Cheyenne and Arapahoe village in eastern Colorado, which had a peace flag flying at the time. The attack resulted in the death and mutilation of some 70 to 163 Indians, mostly unarmed women and children. The location of this unfortunate event is now a historic site administered by the National Park Service. Thirteen years after the Sand Creek attack, on June 25, 1876, the Cheyennes, in collaboration with several other tribes, achieved partial revenge at the Battle of Little Big Horn. This, of course, was the battle during which Lieutenant Colonel George Armstrong Custer was outnumbered, outsmarted and killed.

CHIPETA. Chipeta (pronounced chi-*pee*-tuh), which means White Singing Bird in the Ute language, was the second wife of Ute chief Ouray. She was born in 1843 (or possibly 1844) and died in 1924. After Ouray's death, Chipeta continued her husband's efforts at diplomacy intended to bring peace and tolerance between the Utes and Colorado's white settlers. This was not an easy task in the aftermath of the 1879 Meeker Massacre, which took place not far from where Ouray and Chipeta lived. Chipeta was posthumously inducted into the Colorado Women's Hall of Fame in 1985 as a charter inductee. Among other places in the state, the town of Chipita Park, between Colorado Springs and Woodland Park, was named for her.

COCHETOPA. Cochetopa (pronounced ko-che-*toh*-puh) is a Ute Indian word meaning something like "pass of the buffalo." The name has been given to a pass (10,067 feet) as well as a creek, a hilly grassland region and other places in an area in south-central Colorado that lies roughly between Gunnison on the west and Saguache on the east. Travelers in this area now usually use Colorado Highway 114, which goes over a pass known as North Pass (10,149 feet), because the road there is paved. The road over the original Cochetopa Pass still exists, but it is a gravel county road.

CURECANTI. This name (pronounced koo-reh-*kan*-tee) comes from a Ute Indian chief who apparently liked to hunt and otherwise hang out along the Gunnison River in what is now Curecanti National Recreation Area. (There are numerous iterations of this chief's name, including Currecanti, Curricante and Curicata. The National Park Service, however, chose Curecanti.) The recreation area, partly in Gunnison County and partly in Montrose County, is forty-three thousand acres in size and includes three Gunnison River reservoirs—Blue Mesa (Colorado's largest), Morrow Point and Crystal. Black Canyon of the Gunnison River National Park is adjacent to the recreation area on its westerly (downstream) side.

HURON. This name derives from a North American Indian tribe, more formally known as the Wyandot People. In 1650 or thereabouts (and after having their numbers decimated by diseases imported from Europe), the members of this tribe were chased out of Ontario and split into two groups. One of these groups ended up in Quebec, and the other settled in the Ohio Valley. These Indians made a few bad wartime bets. In the French and Indian War (1754–63), they sided with the French against the British, and the British won. Then, in the American Revolutionary War (1775–83), they sided with the British—and we know what happened there. In 1842, the United States government (perhaps as belated punishment for their having aided the British in the Revolutionary War) relocated what was left of the Ohio Valley group of Hurons to Kansas. Although the Huron Indians did not have a presence in Colorado, the Huron name appears regularly in this state. Huron Peak, in the Sawatch Range in central Colorado, makes it onto the list of Colorado's fourteen-thousand-foot peaks by a mere three feet. It holds position number fifty-two (next to last) on the list. For some reason, this mountain was not officially named by the United States Board on Geographic Names until late in the game, 1956. On July 9, 1994, a Flight for Life helicopter crashed on the side of Huron Peak while trying to rescue an injured hiker. The pilot and flight nurse were killed in the accident.

IDAHO. This name derived from an Apache Indian word meaning "enemy." In the 1850s, the name Idaho was used for an area around what is now the town of Idaho Springs. That town began as the mining camp of an old prospector named George A. Jackson, who discovered gold there in 1859. The town, prior to adopting the name Idaho Springs, was called Jackson's Diggings. The name Idaho seems to have had some marketing appeal, and it was proposed at one point as the name for what became the Colorado Territory. It was then proposed as the name for what became the Washington

Territory, and it finally found a home as the name for the state of Idaho. Idaho Springs sits along Clear Creek in the I-70 corridor and is the county seat for Clear Creek County.

Ignacio. This name (pronounced ig-*nash*-ee-oh) comes from Chief Ignacio (1828–1913) of the Weminuche band of the Ute Indians. Chief Ignacio led his people during trying times when European-American settlers swarming in from the east were pushing the Utes farther and farther away from their native lands. Chief Ignacio, and Chief Ouray of the Uncompahgre band,

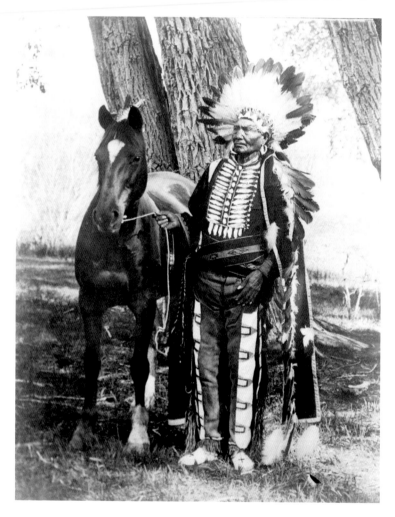

Chief Ignacio of the Weminuche band of the Ute Indians. For better or for worse, a dedicated diplomat for his people. *Library of Congress.*

both traveled to Washington and appeared before Congress in 1880, the year after the Meeker Massacre, in an effort to save as much of their homeland as possible. In the end, most of the Utes were forced out of Colorado and onto a reservation in southeastern Utah. Chief Ignacio, however, managed to keep his band in far southwestern Colorado. The town of Ignacio, on the Colorado portion of the Ute reservation in La Plata County and along the Los Pinos River, is named for him. This town is the capital of the Southern Ute Nation.

KIOWA. This name comes from one of the significant Indian tribes present in Colorado during its formative years. The Kiowa Indians started out in what is now western Montana and migrated into the mountains of what is now Colorado in the 1600s and 1700s and then onto the plains in the early 1800s. At one point in their history, the Kiowas wore a distinctive hairstyle intended to keep their hair from getting tangled up with the arrows they were shooting. (This was apparently an occupational hazard for Indians.) The Kiowas were herded off to a reservation in southwest Oklahoma in 1867. In 1889, Kiowa County, in far eastern Colorado, was created by a carve-out from Bent County (which, in turn, had been carved out of Greenwood County, which no longer exists). The Sand Creek Massacre occurred in what is now Kiowa County in 1864.

MANITOU. *Manitou* is an Indian word meaning "spirit" or perhaps "great spirit." The town of Manitou Springs, which sits between the Garden of the Gods on the east and Pikes Peak on the west (making it the motel capital of the world), was founded by General William Palmer and his business associate, Dr. William Bell, in 1872. The idea was to create a scenic health resort at the foot of Pikes Peak and perhaps also sell train tickets for a ride on General Palmer's Denver and Rio Grande Railway, in which Dr. Bell was an investor. In any event, Manitou Springs claims there are eleven naturally carbonated springs that come to the surface in its midst and that Ute, Cheyenne and other Indian tribes traveled here under an unwritten agreement of peaceful coexistence in pursuit of health benefits associated with these springs. Numerous entrepreneurs have tried to cash in on the purported health benefits of water from the springs, without much success to date. Tourists still flock to the area, however, to give the waters a try, ride the cog railroad to the top of Pikes Peak, visit the Garden of the Gods, buy American Indian jewelry and artifacts (usually made in some foreign country) and otherwise enjoy themselves in the Pikes Peak region.

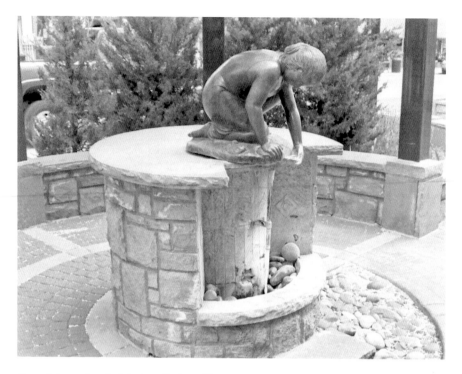

One of the springs in Manitou Springs. There are meant to be eleven of them that can be found on a walk around town. *Photo by author.*

NAVAJO. Colorado has a Navajo Peak (13,409 feet) in the Indian Peaks Range between Boulder and Grand Counties and a Navajo River in Archuleta County in southwest Colorado. The name comes from the Navajo Indian tribe, which is now the most populous (300,000+) tribe recognized by the United States government as a sovereign nation. The Navajos have a large reservation in the Four Corners area, mostly in Arizona and New Mexico, with strikingly beautiful rock formations sprouting up out of the desert. (Note to motorists: Do not speed while on reservation land. The Navajo Nation has its own law enforcement system, which may not always comport with your idea of due process.)

OURAY. The use of this name in Colorado honors Chief Ouray of the Uncompahgre branch of the Ute Indian tribe. The name means "arrow" in the Ute language. Chief Ouray lived from 1833 to 1880. Along the way, he first married Black Mare. After her death, he married White Singing Bird (Chipeta in the Ute language). Chief Ouray learned to speak Spanish and English, as well as the Apache language; he was a champion of peace between

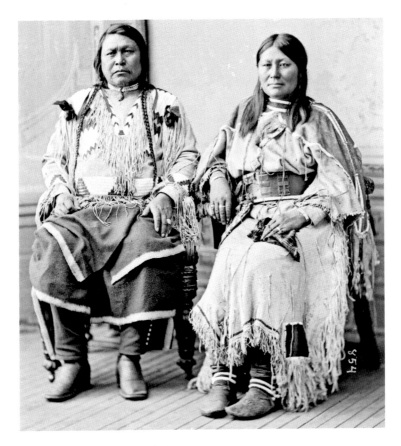

Ouray and Chipita. *Wikimedia Commons.*

the Utes and westward-advancing European-American settlers and was respected by both. In the last year of his life, he went to Washington, D.C., in an attempt to negotiate a treaty with the United States that would allow his people to remain in Colorado. He was unsuccessful in that endeavor, and his part of the Ute tribe ended up being forced to relocate to a reservation that is mostly in Utah. Ouray County was formed in 1877, and the city of Ouray (what there is of it) was formed in 1884. In another of Colorado's frequent county shuffles, Ouray County was renamed Uncompahgre County for four days in 1883. The state legislature then changed its mind and restored the original name. Ouray County is in southwest Colorado and is tucked away in a beautiful part of the San Juan Mountains, causing it to be known as the Switzerland of America.

PAGOSA. This name is derived from a Ute Indian word meaning "boiling waters." However, promoters of the town of Pagosa Springs, in Archuleta County on the west side of Wolf Creek Pass, spun this into "healing waters." In any event, the town got its name because of the hot springs in the area. Pagosa Springs is the county seat for, and the only incorporated municipality in, Archuleta County.

PAWNEE. The Pawnees were an Indian tribe living, farming and hunting in and around the Great American Desert, including the eastern plains of Colorado, until they were chased out by settlers moving west. Most members of what is left of the Pawnee tribe now live on a reservation in Oklahoma, where they operate casinos and dodge tornados. In Colorado, we have Pawnee Buttes in Weld County and Pawnee Peak (12,943 feet) in the Indian Peaks Range between Grand and Boulder Counties.

PICEANCE. The current best guess as to the origin of this name is that it's a derivation of a Shoshoni Indian word meaning "tall grass." Notwithstanding the spelling, the preferred pronunciation seems to be "*pee-ance.*" In northwest Colorado, we have Piceance Creek, a fifty-eight-mile tributary of the White River (with no fish), and the Piceance Basin, an important geologic area with proven reserves of coal, natural gas and oil shale. Piceance Creek runs parallel to the eastern flank of the Roan Plateau, and the controversial oil and gas development activity in this area is very apparent as you drive along the creek on Rio Blanco County Road 5.

SAGUACHE. This name (properly pronounced sah-*watch*, although you will certainly hear variations on the theme) comes from a Ute Indian word meaning "water at blue earth." This was catchy enough to earn naming rights to a county in south-central Colorado in 1866, ten years before Colorado became a state. The land forming this county, in another of Colorado's many county boundary line shuffles, was taken from Lake County and Costilla County. Agricultural activities in the county really took off in the 1870s when gold and silver were discovered in the nearby Sangre de Cristo Range, and miners found it useful to have food to eat. Saguache County boasts that it is home to Colorado's smallest incorporated town, Bonanza, and that although the county has one thousand miles of roads, it has no stop lights. The county seat—the town of Saguache—was incorporated in 1891 and doesn't look much different today than it did then, although the plumbing may now be better.

SAWATCH. This is another spelling, or perhaps misspelling, of Saguache and is the spelling that made it into the naming of a major subrange of Colorado's highest mountains, lying west of the U.S. Highway 285 corridor between Salida and Leadville. Fifteen of Colorado's fourteeners are in the Sawatch Range, including Colorado's highest peak, Mount Elbert. This spelling, compared to Saguache, is more likely to result in a correct pronunciation of the word.

SHAVANO. Shavano (18??–1885) (pronounced *shah*-van-oh) was a chief of the Tabeguache band of the Ute Indian tribe from the 1850s through the 1870s. He believed his tribe had no choice but to make peace with the white man, and he regularly took that position, no doubt to the occasional dismay of his people. Chief Shavano's efforts at peace included signing two treaties with the United States government, the second of which required a trip to Washington, D.C. Shavano is credited with helping to obtain the release of the family of Indian agent Nathan Meeker in the aftermath of the Meeker Massacre of 1879. Meeker and several members of his staff had been killed by a renegade group of Utes, and Meeker's family was taken prisoner. Showing no appreciation for his peacekeeping efforts, the United States, in 1881, herded Chief Shavano and his band of the Ute tribe off to a reservation in the deserts of Utah. Shavano died there in 1885. Mount Shavano, in the Sawatch Range in central Colorado, is the state's seventeenth-highest peak at 14,229 feet. It is one of three Colorado fourteeners in what is known as the Indian Group mountains. The other two are Antero and Tabeguache. These three mountains sit side by side in dramatic fashion on the west side of the Upper Arkansas River Valley between Buena Vista and Salida.

TABEGUACHE. This name (pronounced *tab*-uh-watch) comes from a band of Ute Indians that was present in Colorado when the European-American invasion began. The Utes were never a unified people. Instead, they were divided into numerous separate groups that maintained affiliations with varying degrees of closeness. Tabeguache Peak tops out at 14,155 feet, is one of the three mountains making up the Indian Group (the others being Shavano and Antero) in central Colorado and holds twenty-fifth place on Colorado's list of fourteeners.

TAHAMA. Tahama (pronounced ta-*hah*-ma) was a Sioux Indian chief and scout who traveled with Zebulon Pike during at least some of his wanderings around Colorado. A spring located in what is now Monument Valley Park in Colorado Springs was named after Tahama. General William Palmer, the

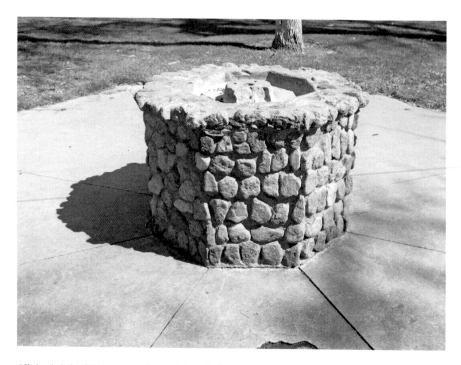

All that's left of Tahama springs, Colorado Springs' only original spring. *Photo by author.*

founder of Colorado Springs, apparently knew of this spring and at some point expressed a desire that it be named for Tahama. This finally happened around 1926, when a small but elegant pavilion was built at the site of the spring as part of a commemoration of Colorado's fiftieth anniversary as a state. Unfortunately, the pavilion took a hit in a tremendous flood that tore through Monument Valley Park in 1935. It took another hit when a second flood struck the area in 1965. This led to removal of the structure, and now only a small stone mound marks the site and caps the spring, leaving Colorado Springs without any actual functioning original spring.

Tomichi. In 1776, the Dominguez-Escalante expedition (which was looking for a route from Santa Fe to the Spanish missions in California but never made it to California) reported this as the name (pronounced toh-*mee*-chee) given by Ute Indians to the Gunnison River. That didn't stick, but the name lives on with a fishy-looking creek that runs along U.S. Highway 50 from the west side of Monarch Pass to the town of Gunnison. Unfortunately, most of Tomichi Creek is on private land, so fishermen can only stare and wonder. One theory about the name has it that *tomichi* is a Ute Indian word meaning "hot" or "boiling" and that its use came about because of the hot springs to be found in what is now Gunnison County. Another theory, however, is that "tomichi" came from a similar-sounding Ute Indian word meaning "dome-shaped rock." Such a rock—actually, a dome-shaped mountain called Tomichi Dome (11,465 feet)—exists north of U.S. Highway 50 and east of the town of Gunnison.

UNAWEEP. This name (pronounced *yoo*-nah-weep) is derived from a Ute Indian word, but no one is too sure which one or what it meant. One theory has it that the name means "fire canyon" and was given to a canyon in Mesa County, in far western Colorado, because of the red color predominant in the canyon. Another theory says the name means "canyon with two mouths." In that regard, Unaweep Canyon, in addition to being picturesque, is unique in that it's the only canyon in the world having a divide in the middle, causing streams to run out of it in different directions at each end. The name of these streams doesn't show much imagination but gets the point across. East Creek flows east to the Gunnison River. West Creek flows west to the Dolores River. The barely perceptible Unaweep Divide, which causes this watershed phenomenon, tops out at 7,008 feet. Colorado Highway 141 runs through Unaweep Canyon and is part of the Unaweep/Tabeguache Scenic Byway.

UNCOMPAHGRE. This is a Ute Indian word (pronounced un-kum-*pah*-gruh) variously translated into English as "dirty water," "red water spring" and "hot water spring." All of these names relate to an abundance of natural hot springs in the west-central part of Colorado. The water from these springs, although perhaps nice to sit in on a cold winter day, doesn't taste very good and sometimes has a reddish color. In one of Colorado's many county shuffles, Ouray County was named Uncompahgre County for four days in 1883. Uncompahgre Peak, at 14,309 feet, is Colorado's sixth-highest mountain and the highest mountain in the San Juan Range. It is a dramatic and easily identified sight when cruising into Lake City northbound over Slumgullion Pass on Colorado Highway 149.

UTE. This name has been given to lots of places in Colorado and, of course, comes from the Ute Indians. The Ute Indians, before being herded off to three reservations in Colorado and Utah, were originally to be found in large expanses of western Colorado and eastern Utah, as well as parts of New Mexico and Wyoming. The Utes were not a unified tribe. Instead, there were multiple separate bands roaming around and maintaining alliances with varying degrees of closeness. The name Utah was derived from the name Ute. In the tribal language, *ute* means "land of the sun."

Weminuche. This name (pronounced weh-mih-*noo*-chi) comes from one of the bands of the Ute Indian tribe. The Utes had a significant presence in the Four Corners area (southwestern Colorado, eastern Utah, northern Arizona and northwestern New Mexico) for many hundreds of years before Spanish conquistadors, missionaries, fur trappers, gold seekers, buffalo hunters, land speculators, politicians and others messed things up for them. The name may relate back to an ancient Indian word meaning "canyon people." The Weminuche Wilderness Area, at 488,210 acres, is the largest federal wilderness area in Colorado. Part of the Weminuche Wilderness Area is in the San Juan National Forest, and another part is in the Rio Grande National Forest. Jumping-off points for backpacking adventures into this spectacular part of southwestern Colorado include Durango and Silverton.

Yampa. This name comes from an Indian word for a plant (a member of the parsley family) that is still present, and once was abundant, in northwest Colorado. It was an important food source for Indian tribes living in the area. The roots, when cooked, apparently have a crunchy texture and are mildly sweet, resembling water chestnuts. (Beware, however, that when eaten raw and in excess, they become a laxative, something the Indians also figured out.) The Yampa River is one of Colorado's major rivers, with its headwaters just east of the small town of Yampa, in Routt County. The river then flows westerly through Steamboat Springs and continues on to a confluence with the Green River (a tributary of the Colorado River) at Dinosaur National Monument, near the Utah border. The river's total length is some 250 miles.

Yuma. This name comes from the Quechan (Yuma) nation, an Indian tribe that populated the Southwest long before the arrival of invaders from Spain or the eastern United States. What's left of the tribe now resides on the Fort Yuma Indian Reservation along the lower Colorado River. Part of this reservation is in Arizona, and part is in California. In Colorado, Yuma County, in the northeast corner of the state, was formed in 1889 out of land taken from Washington County. There isn't much Yuma County is known for other than the fact that it contains the lowest elevation point in Colorado, which, nonetheless, is the highest low elevation point of any state in the country.

CHAPTER 3

EXPLORERS, MOUNTAIN MEN AND SOLDIERS

Many Colorado place names came from the brave (or possibly crazy) individuals who helped to explore and map Colorado in the 1800s. These individuals were often encouraged in their efforts by the United States Congress, which wanted to know what it got for its money with the 1803 impulse shopping event known as the Louisiana Purchase. Congress also wasn't too sure what it got in 1848 with the Treaty of Guadalupe Hidalgo, which ended the Mexican-American War and transferred to the United States ownership of most of what are now the southwestern states, including a substantial part of Colorado. Congress was additionally eager to connect the West Coast and the East Coast by rail service and by telegraph, and it created generous economic incentives for explorers in pursuit of those goals.

All of this led to several federally funded expeditions, starting with Zebulon Pike's foray into Colorado, which began in 1806 and continued into 1807. (Pike himself could have used some better maps—or possibly GPS—since he mistakenly established a camp in territory claimed by Spain and was promptly hauled off to New Mexico by Spanish soldiers and held captive there for four months.)

After Pike, we had Major Stephen H. Long, who in 1820 led an expedition into Colorado that traveled from what is now Rocky Mountain National Park south to the Arkansas River. Long had with him not only soldiers but also scientists and artists, and this allowed for the accumulation of much new knowledge about the geology, flora and fauna of the Colorado mountains. A group of five men from Long's party, led by Edwin James but not including

Long himself, achieved the first recorded ascent of Pikes Peak. (Zebulon Pike started up the Great Mountain, as he called it, but concluded it was unclimbable and turned back before he and his men froze to death.)

John C. Frémont also deserves mention here for his march through Colorado in 1845, on the third of his expeditions exploring the western United States. The same goes for John W. Gunnison, a member of the Corps of Topographical Engineers, who was killed by Indians in 1853 while looking for a transcontinental rail route that would cross Colorado.

Additional excursions of note were four federally funded exploring and mapping expeditions that took place between 1869 and 1879 and came to be known as the Great Surveys. These expeditions were led by Ferdinand Hayden, John Wesley Powell, George Wheeler and Clarence King, and they provided the first detailed and reliable maps of the western half of Colorado, as well as other parts of the American West. Clarence King in particular rose to fame during this era and became the first director of the United States Geological Survey, occupying that position from 1879 to 1881. John Wesley Powell succeeded him and directed the agency for thirteen years, from 1881 to 1894.

Prior to the Great Surveys, hordes of men (and a few women) were exploring Colorado's mountains in search of rail routes and gold, and before that, there were the mountain men. The mountain men were poking around remote regions of Colorado from 1810 through midcentury as part of a highly organized assault on the resident beaver population, backed in that enterprise by large corporations such as the Hudson Bay Company and John Jacob Astor's American Fur Company. When the beavers grew scarce and European fashion trends switched from beaver hats to silk hats, many of the mountain men hung around and found jobs as scouts and guides, furthering the exploration and mapping of Colorado.

The military presence in Colorado has also played an important role in the naming of places in this state. The assigned duties of military officers in the nineteenth century often included exploration. And as the European-American westward migration gained momentum, a military presence was necessary to protect travelers to, and settlers in, the Colorado Territory from attacks by Indians. Indian hostilities from 1863 to 1865 gave rise to what became known as the Colorado War, wherein the Cheyenne and Arapahoe tribes—and to a lesser extent the Kiowa, Comanche and Sioux tribes—fought bitter battles with settlers, a Colorado Territorial Militia and the United States Army over rights to land the Indians thought had been promised to them in treaties.

In sum, throughout Colorado's years of exploration, names were being given to mountains, lakes, rivers and towns, and those names are still with us today. And as for the military, its presence in Colorado left its mark on this state's place names during the last half of the nineteenth century, and that influence has continued through the present day, in particular in the Colorado Spring area, where military bases—the United States Air Force Academy, Fort Carson, Schriever Air Force Base, Peterson Air Force Base and Cheyenne Mountain—are vital to the local economy.

———•———

BERTHOUD. This name, given to a mountain pass and a town, among other things, honors the accomplishments of Captain Edward Louis Berthoud (1828–1910). Berthoud was born in Switzerland, grew up in upstate New York and ended up settling in Golden, Colorado, after a stint as a surveyor involved in the construction of the Panama Canal. He served in the Union army during the Civil War and as a member of the Colorado legislature. He was also the first registrar at the Colorado School of Mines. Berthoud is best known for his surveying work for the Colorado Central Railroad. He and mountain man Jim Bridger are credited with discovering what is now Berthoud Pass, a mountain pass crossing the Continental Divide linking the Winter Park ski area with Interstate 70. The highway in question is U.S. Highway 40. Berthoud Pass tops out at 11,307 feet, placing it thirteenth on the list of Colorado mountain passes with an improved road (paved or gravel) on both sides.

BIERSTADT. Albert Bierstadt (1830–1902) was one of the preeminent landscape painters working in Colorado in the last half of the nineteenth century. He was born in Germany but came to America when he was one year old. He later returned to Germany to study painting. Before coming west, he worked in eastern New York State and was part of a group of artists associated with a style of painting that became known as the Hudson River School. In 1914, twelve years after his death, Bierstadt had a mountain named after him. Mount Bierstadt is a Front Range peak that, at 14,060 feet, holds thirty-eighth place on the list of Colorado's fourteeners. Bierstadt may have actually participated in the first recorded ascent of this mountain.

BIJOU. There are two small communities in Colorado, both east of the mountains, named Bijou. One is in Elbert County and the other in Morgan

County. There is also a Bijou Creek, which begins in Adams County and flows eastward some forty-five miles to its confluence with the South Platte River near Fort Morgan, and a Bijou Street in Colorado Springs. *Bijou* is the French word for "jewel," so that might explain the use of the name (although neither of these towns nor the creek nor the street would seem to qualify as a jewel). More likely, the name came from a well-known French trapper and guide named Joseph Bijeau, who accompanied the 1820 expedition of Major Stephen H. Long into Colorado and whose name was occasionally misspelled as Bijou.

BRIDGER. James Felix Bridger (1804–1881) is perhaps the most famous mountain man, explorer, trapper, guide and Indian negotiator of all time. Bridger roamed the West from southern Colorado to the Canadian border for more than fifty years, beginning in the 1820s. Along the way, he is credited with being one of the first explorers to see and report about the geothermal activity at what is now Yellowstone National Park and to visit the Great Salt Lake (which, because of its salinity, he thought was the Pacific Ocean). Bridger married three Indian women during his life, each of whom bore him children. He founded Fort Bridger, Wyoming, as a private entrepreneurial undertaking, and shortly before his death, he made an unsuccessful attempt to collect rent from the United States Army for its use of this property. All manner of well-known places throughout the West are named after Bridger. As a snippet of Jim Bridger trivia, one of his rifles is a traveling trophy given to the winner each year of the Utah State University/University of Wyoming football game, now known as "Bridger's Battle."

BUCKLEY. This name comes from First Lieutenant John Harold Buckley. He was from Longmont and had the misfortune of being killed in France during World War I. Buckley Field was established early in World War II as a Colorado Air National Guard base.

CAPITOL. Capitol Peak, at 14,130 feet, ranks twenty-ninth on the list of Colorado's 14,000-foot mountains. The name was given to the mountain by the U.S. government's Hayden Survey of 1874. It's not known if any deep thought went into the naming of the peak. Perhaps the shape of the mountain reminded the survey party members of state capitol building with which they were familiar. Members of the Hayden Survey did not climb this peak, unlike most others encountered during the expedition, considering it inaccessible. This may have been a wise decision since Capitol Peak still wins the prize as the most difficult of the Colorado fourteeners to climb. The only non-technical route to the summit requires crossing the "Knife Edge," which, as the name implies, is a super-narrow ridge allowing no room for error. The technical routes to the summit (requiring ropes, pitons, crampons, prayer books and other climbing essentials) are problematic as well because of loose rocks that can come crashing down on climbers.

CARSON. This name comes from Christopher Houston "Kit" Carson (1809–1868), a famous (or infamous, depending on your point of view) explorer, trapper, mountain man, scout (for John C. Frémont's explorations into California and Oregon), military officer and Indian fighter. During his

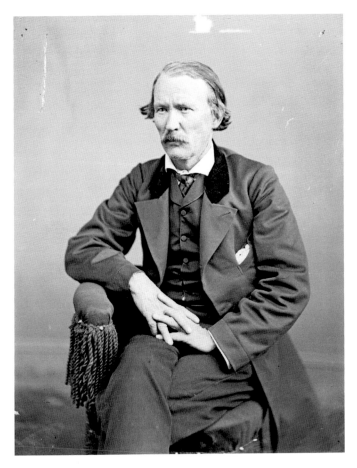

Christopher Kit Carson, the only general in the history of the U.S. military who couldn't read or write. *Library of Congress.*

trapper days, he lived among the Arapaho and Cheyenne Indian tribes. In 1835, at age twenty-five, he married Singing Grass, an Arapaho. This followed an on-horseback shootout with another admirer of Singing Grass, a French Canadian trapper named Joseph Chouinard. This event occurred at a mountain man rendezvous along the Green River in what is now southwestern Wyoming. Carson and Chouinard each came close to killing the other, but both survived, with Singing Grass apparently deciding Carson was the better catch. After their marriage, she traveled with him all over the Rocky Mountains in pursuit of, presumably, beaver pelts. Singing Grass died sometime between 1838 and 1840 after giving birth to a second child. In 1840, Carson married a Cheyenne Indian woman named Making-Our-Road. (This no doubt sounded better in the Cheyenne language.) Making-Our-Road dumped Carson after a year, deciding to follow her tribe on its next migration rather than follow her husband. Carson married a third time in 1843. This time his wife was fourteen years old and Hispanic. Her name was Joseta Jaramillo. Joseta bore Carson eight children, and Carson relatives from this marriage are still to be found in Colorado. Carson fought for the Union in the Civil War and thereafter in campaigns against several different Indian tribes. He is believed to be the only military officer in the history of the United States rising to the rank of general who could not read or write. A sparsely populated county on the far eastern side of Colorado was named for Carson in 1889. This county was a carve-out from adjacent Elbert County. Kit Carson Peak, in the Sangre de Cristo Range, is Colorado's twenty-third highest mountain, at 14,165 feet. Fort Carson, a 137,000-acre army base adjacent to Colorado Springs, was also named for General Carson.

CHALLENGER. Challenger Point, a prominence along the northwest shoulder of Kit Carson Peak in the Sangre de Cristo Range in south-central Colorado, was given its name in 1987 in honor of the seven members of the crew of the space shuttle *Challenger* who died when the shuttle exploded shortly after takeoff on January 28, 1986. A plaque was installed on Challenger Point in 1987 that reads: "In memory of the crew of shuttle *Challenger*—seven who died accepting the risk, expanding mankind's horizons." The plaque ends with a Latin phrase, *"Ad astra per aspera,"* meaning something like "To the stars through adversity," followed by the date of the accident. Challenger Point apparently meets the "prominence" test. That is, it sits at least 300 feet above the saddle connecting it to slightly higher Kit Carson Peak, thereby allowing it to have the status of a separate fourteener. At 14,081 feet, it ranks thirty-fourth on the fourteener list.

COLLINS. This name comes from Colonel William O. Collins, who was the commandant of Fort Laramie, Wyoming, in 1864 when an army post was established at the current site of the city of Fort Collins. The Cache La Poudre River, both a blessing (recreation and irrigation) and a curse (occasional flooding), runs through Fort Collins. Fort Collins is Colorado's fourth-largest city by population, the county seat of Larimer County and the home of Colorado State University. The Walt Disney Company used Fort Collins (and Marceline, Missouri) as a model when designing the "main street" attractions at its various theme parks.

CROOK. This name comes from Major General George R. Crook (1830–1890) and has nothing to do with criminal behavior (although there was plenty of that going on in Colorado in the second half of the nineteenth century). In 1881 or thereabouts, the Union Pacific Railroad gave this name to a town along its tracks in Logan County, in the northeast part of the state. After the Civil War, General Crook commanded troops in this area—at the time known as the "Indian Frontier"—and the railroad was presumably appreciative of his efforts to keep its employees and customers safe from Indian attack.

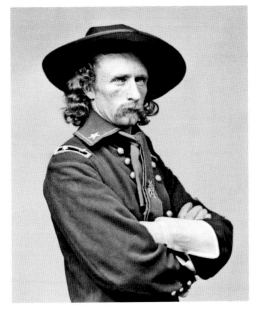

CUSTER. This name comes from Lieutenant Colonel George Armstrong Custer (1839–1876) who, after a distinguished but little-known military career, managed to become famous by having one really bad day in 1876, the same year Colorado became a state. Custer County, in south-central Colorado, was formed the following year, in 1877, by a carve-out from Fremont County. Custer County is a spectacular bit of geography, with the Wet Mountains to the east, the Sangre de Cristo Range to the west and the lush Wet Mountain Valley in

George Armstrong Custer, of "Custer's Last Stand" fame. *Wikimedia Commons.*

between. A silver rush in 1870 helped to populate the area. Westcliffe, a funky little town with starter castle vacation homes nearby and good art galleries, is the county seat for Custer County.

ELLINGWOOD. This name comes from Albert R. Ellingwood (1888–1934). Ellingwood was a pioneering member of the Colorado Mountain Club and one of the first to climb all of Colorado's fourteen-thousand-foot peaks. One of those peaks, Ellingwood Point, bears his name. Ellingwood Point is a short distance from Blanca Peak, and the two are often climbed together by people who like this sort of thing. (At Ellingwood's birth, it seemed unlikely he would grow up to be a famous mountaineer since he was born in Iowa.) Ellingwood was a Rhodes scholar, taught political science for a time at Colorado College and was an assistant dean at Northwestern University at the time of his death.

ENT. This name comes from Major General Uzal Girard Ent (1900–1948), who, beginning in 1943, commanded a tent city in Colorado Springs established in connection with the construction of an air force base that was then given his name. In 1944, Major General Ent was seriously injured in the crash of a B52 bomber on takeoff. He received a disability discharge due to his injuries and died four years later. From 1957 to 1963, the Ent facility was the home of the North American Aerospace Defense Command (NORAD, known as the North American Air Defense Command until 1981). Since the late 1970s, the Ent location has been a United States Olympic Committee training center. The USOC also had its administrative headquarters there until it moved them to downtown Colorado Springs in 2010.

FITZSIMONS. This name comes from Lieutenant William Thomas Fitzsimons (1889–1917). He was a physician and had the bad luck to be the first U.S. Army officer killed in World War I. Fitzsimons Army Medical Center in Denver was named in his honor. Its most famous patient was President Dwight Eisenhower, who spent time there in 1955 recovering from a heart attack. The army facility closed in 1999 and, through redevelopment, has morphed into the Anschutz Medical Campus.

FREMONT. The name Fremont, as used throughout Colorado (and elsewhere), recognizes the accomplishments (or lack thereof) of John Charles Frémont (1813–1890). Frémont was an American military officer, an explorer, an entrepreneur and a politician, a somewhat unusual skill set. History has given him mixed reviews. He served as the military governor of California during the Mexican-American War. He was one of California's first two senators when California became a state in 1850. He was the Republican Party candidate for president in 1856 but lost to Democrat James Buchanan. He acquired a great deal of real estate–related wealth during the California gold rush days but, along the way, planted the seeds for years of litigation over landownership, some of which went all the way to the United States Supreme Court. After the Civil War, during which he had good days and bad, Frémont lost most of his wealth thanks to soured investments, including a failed railroad venture. He died destitute in New York in 1890. Fremont County, in south-central Colorado, was named after General Frémont in 1861, when Colorado became a territory. It was one of the original seventeen counties making up the Colorado Territory. In 1877, Fremont County lost some of its land to Custer County. Fremont County is best known for prisons. It has something like fifteen of them, including the Colorado State Penitentiary in Cañon City and the United States' only federal Supermax facility in Florence.

FRYINGPAN. The Fryingpan River got its name after a group of trappers was attacked by a band of Ute Indians. All but two of the trappers were killed, and one of the survivors was badly injured. The injured man hid in a cave along the river, and the remaining survivor went for help. Before leaving his wounded colleague, he placed a frying pan in a tree to mark the location of the cave. When he returned, the frying pan was still there and the cave was located, but the injured man was dead. The Fryingpan River has its headwaters on the west side of the Continental Divide in the Sawatch Range mountains. It flows westerly some forty-two miles to its confluence with the Roaring Fork River, north of Aspen and south of Glenwood Springs. Along the way, the river is dammed and fills Ruedi Reservoir. The river coming out of the reservoir is a famous fly-fishing tail water, although (in my limited experience) the fish there routinely outsmart the fishermen. Upstream of the reservoir, water is taken out of the river and shipped over the mountains to the Arkansas River, where it provides a multitude of Front Range water users with an additional source of water. The Fryingpan/Arkansas Project was approved by President Kennedy in 1962 after fifty years of controversy. Ruedi Reservoir was included in the project as a way to compensate western slope water users for the water that was lost to (or, to their mind, stolen by) Front Range users.

GORE. This name comes from Sir St. George Gore (1811–1878). Gore was an Irish nobleman (the baronet of Gore Manor in County Donegal). Having lots of money, nothing better to do and perhaps having already killed off all the wildlife in his neck of the woods, Gore, from 1854 to 1857, roamed around the mountains of the West shooting things. He boasted of killing 2,000 buffalo, 1,600 deer and elk and 100 bears, just for sport. And this was no rough-it-in-the-wilderness expedition. Gore brought along with him a large, colorfully decorated tent, complete with furniture; twenty-seven vehicles; 100 horses; 18 oxen; and a support staff of forty, including mountain man Jim Bridger as a guide. In appreciation for this senseless slaughter, Gore managed to get a mountain range and a mountain pass named after him. The Gore Range runs for sixty miles through north-central Colorado. Its highest elevation is the summit of Mount Powell, at 13,566 feet. The Gore Range is clearly (and beautifully) visible from Silverthorne to Vail along Interstate 70. Gore Pass (9,527 feet) crosses the Gorge Range on its north side. It is traversed by paved Colorado Highway 134, which connects an area near Kremmling on the east with the Yampa River Valley on the west.

GRAY. This name comes from Asa Gray (1810–1888), a botanist. His name was given to Grays Peak by another botanist and colleague, Charles C. Parry. Parry made the first reported climb of the mountain in 1861. Asa Gray didn't actually see the mountain bearing his name for another eleven years, until 1872. Grays Peak, north and west a bit from Denver, is, at 14,270 feet, the ninth-highest mountain in Colorado and is the highest mountain in the area known as the Front Range. It also has the distinction of being the highest point along the Continental Divide in all of North America.

GUNNISON. This name comes from John Williams Gunnison (1812–1853), an army officer who was part of the Corps of Topographical Engineers and who, after assignments in Florida and around the Great Lakes, was charged with looking for a route for a transcontinental railroad through what eventually became Colorado and Utah. While on that assignment, in 1853, he was killed by a group of Pahvant Ute Indians. There is mystery and intrigue here. Credible evidence apparently exists that Brigham Young and the Mormon Church, by now having established a substantial presence in Utah, were behind Gunnison's murder. In any event, Gunnison County, formed in 1876 when Colorado became a state, was named after him, as was the town of Gunnison and the Gunnison River. Gunnison County is in west-central Colorado, and although it's one of the coldest places on the planet in winter, it is a hotspot for mountain recreation, including fishing, hunting, mountain climbing and skiing at the Crested Butte ski area.

HALE. This name comes from Brigadier General Irving Hale (1861–1930), a West Point graduate who led troops from Colorado deployed in the Philippines during the Spanish-American War. (In case you've forgotten, the Spanish-American War grew out of a revolution in Cuba intended to remove Spanish rule from that country. The United States decided to take sides and ended up engaged in military operations both in Cuba and the Philippines.) Camp Hale, in the Eagle River Valley between Leadville and Red Cliff, was established in 1942 as headquarters for the Tenth Mountain Division, whose soldiers were trained to, and did, fight on skis during World War II. Many of the members of the Tenth Mountain Division returned to Colorado after the war and became active in developing Colorado's ski industry.

HANDIES. Handies Peak, in the San Juan Mountains in southwest Colorado, at 14,048 feet, holds fortieth place on the list of Colorado's highest mountains. There is no clear history as to the origin of the name. The mountain already had this name when the United States government's Hayden Survey arrived on the scene in 1874 and proceeded to assign names to other mountains. One commonly held theory is that the name came from an early pioneer/mountaineer/surveyor who lived in the Lake City area during the middle years of the nineteenth century (and was not eaten by Alfred Packer, Colorado's best-known cannibal, who also hung out in the Lake City area).

HAYDEN. This name comes from Ferdinand Vandeveer Hayden (1829–1887). Hayden, a geologist and a physician, eventually became head of the U.S. Geological and Geographical Survey of the Territories. He led one of the four surveys (known as the "Great Surveys") commissioned by Congress in the 1860s and 1870s intended to determine just what the west was all about. Back then, easterners still weren't sure about this, and rumors and storytelling were rampant. Hayden's work included time in Colorado and the naming of, and first climbs of, many of Colorado's mountains. There is a small town in Routt County, along U.S. Highway 40, named after Hayden. Despite a population under two thousand, Hayden, because of its proximity to Steamboat Springs, has an airport (airport code HDN) serving several commercial airlines during the ski season. Hayden Pass, in Fremont County in the vicinity of Salida, crosses over a part of the Sangre de Cristo Range and connects the Arkansas River Valley with the San Luis Valley. There is a 15.8-mile, sometimes 4x4-only, road across the pass, which tops out at 10,709 feet.

KING. Clarence Rivers King (1842–1901) was a Yale-educated geologist and mountaineer who became the first director of the United States Geological Survey, a post he held from 1879 to 1881. King spent time in Colorado in connection with the 1867 Geological Survey of the Fortieth Parallel, one of the four Great Surveys of the western United States. King also helped to expose one of the boldest financial frauds of the nineteenth century—the Great Diamond Hoax of 1872—which involved the seeding of a remote area in northwest Colorado with cheap diamond fragments purchased in Europe for something like $35,000. The fraudsters were a couple of luckless prospectors from Kentucky named Phil Arnold and John Slack, who decided there was an easier way to riches than prospecting. They sold their worthless diamond mine claims to a syndicate made up of some very sophisticated financiers from San Francisco and New York (Rothschild, Tiffany and Greeley, among others) for $660,000. Neither Arnold nor Slack was ever successfully prosecuted for this crime. Arnold later became a banker back in Kentucky and eventually settled a civil lawsuit brought against him by one of the defrauded investors for $150,000. He died of complications from a wound suffered in a gunfight with another banker. Slack became a casket maker in New Mexico and lived a quiet life until his death in 1896, at age seventy-six, from natural causes. Although you would think Clarence King deserved to have a fourteener named after him, that didn't happen. All he got was a modest mountain in Routt County, south of Steamboat Springs, which is now part of a twelve-thousand-acre Bureau of Land Management recreation area known as the King Mountain Area (no motorized vehicles allowed).

LARAMIE. Although this name shows up in Wyoming more often than in Colorado, the Laramie River has its headwaters in north-central Colorado and is therefore considered one of Colorado's many rivers. The name comes from a French Canadian fur trapper named Jacques La Ramée (1780–circa 1820), who settled in what is now Wyoming sometime around 1815. La Ramée went off on one of his fur hunting trips in 1820 (or possibly 1821) and never came back. There were suspicions that he had been killed by a band of Arapaho Indians living or hunting in the area, but the Indians adamantly denied any involvement in his death. Anyone having knowledge about this possible unsolved homicide should contact local authorities.

LINDSEY. Malcolm Lindsey (1880–1951), who grew up in Trinidad, Colorado, was an avid and active member of the Colorado Mountain Club and served as its president from 1943 to 1946. His favorite 14,000-foot mountain, in the Sangre de Cristo Range not far from Trinidad, was originally named Old Baldy. However, in 1953, the mountain was renamed Mount Lindsey in his honor. This name change was submitted to and approved by a branch of the United States government you may never have heard of: the U.S. Board on Geographic Names. Mount Lindsey, at 14,042 feet, ranks forty-third on the list of Colorado fourteeners. A memorial plaque was installed at the foot of Mount Lindsey in May 1955. However, the plaque was stolen within a month and never recovered.

LONG. The name Long as used in Colorado recognizes the accomplishments of Major Stephen Harriman Long (1784–1864). Long was born in New Hampshire, attended Dartmouth College and went on to be a prolific explorer in the employ of the U.S. Army. He led five expeditions into the hinterland, covering something like twenty-six thousand square miles. One of his expeditions gets credit for the first sighting of Longs Peak, on June 30, 1820. Longs Peak, a Front Range mountain with an elevation of 14,255 feet, ranks number fifteen on the list of Colorado's highest peaks. On one of his expeditions into the central plains, Long described what he saw as a "great desert." That statement gave rise to the Great American Desert nickname this part of the country has been stuck with ever since. The city of Longmont, in Boulder and Weld Counties, takes its name from Longs Peak and, therefore, Stephen Long.

MARSHALL. This name comes from Lieutenant William L. Marshall, a member of the 1873 U.S. Government Wheeler Survey. Lieutenant Marshall, one of the hardy folks involved in this part of the Great Surveys, discovered a pass connecting Salida to Gunnison, and the pass, which rises to 10,843 feet, bears Lieutenant Marshall's name. At the time of this discovery, Lieutenant Marshall was suffering from a painful toothache and was hustling back to Denver to get help. Marshall Pass lies only a few miles to the south of Monarch Pass and was given serious consideration as the route U.S. Highway 50 should take over the Continental Divide between Salida and Gunnison. Monarch Pass, however, won out. A narrow-gauge railroad formerly traversed Marshall Pass. Today, there is a gravel road over the pass allowing summer access by passenger vehicles whose owners aren't overly concerned about suspension component wear. At one time, there was a small settlement along the pass, also known as Marshall Pass. In 1948, *TIME* magazine declared this to be the country's smallest community—population eleven—having an officially designated post office.

MORGAN. The name Morgan comes from a fort established in northeast Colorado along the Overland Trail in the 1860s. Soldiers were stationed at this fort to protect people and stagecoach freight moving through the area on their way to and from destinations to the west, as far away as Oregon. The Overland Trail had its beginning in Atchison, Kansas, and eventually connected to the Oregon Trail at Fort Bridger, in southwest Wyoming. Fort Morgan was originally named Camp Wardwell, but the name was changed in 1866 in memory of Colonel Christopher A. Morgan, an army officer of no great fame who died earlier that year. The fort was shut down in 1869. The town of Fort Morgan was chartered in 1884, and Morgan County was created in 1889 out of land taken from Weld County. The town of Fort Morgan is the county seat of Morgan County.

OXFORD. This name comes to Colorado from Oxford University in England. Mount Oxford, which at 14,153 feet ranks twenty-sixth on the

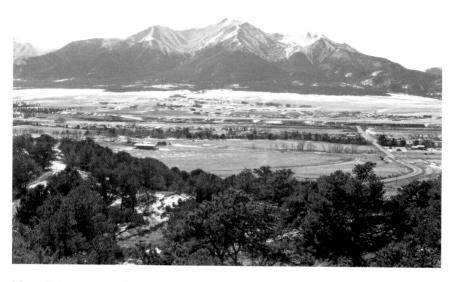

Mount Princeton, one of the magnificent Collegiate Range peaks, as seen from the east side of the Upper Arkansas River Valley. *Photo by author.*

list of Colorado's highest mountains, is one of a group of five fourteeners in the Sawatch Range of central Colorado known (for obvious reasons) as the Collegiate Peaks. The other four are Harvard, Princeton, Yale and Columbia. Mount Oxford was not named until 1925, having seemingly been overlooked in prior surveys of mountain summits and name assignments. The name finally came from John L. Jerome Hart, who wrote a detailed history of the Colorado fourteeners in 1925 in which he assigned the Oxford name to the peak. John Hart and his brother, Stephen Hart, another prominent mountaineer of the era, both attended Oxford University. Mount Oxford was the last of Colorado's original fifty-two fourteeners to be given its current official name. Challenger Point was added in 1986, bringing the total to fifty-three.

PETERSON. Peterson Air Force Base is a military facility that began life as U.S. Army Air Base, Peterson Field, and later, when the United States Air Force got going and the army bowed out of aviation, it became an air force complex. The base shares runways with the Colorado Springs Municipal Airport. The original runways were completed in early August 1942, and on August 8, 1942, First Lieutenant Edward J. Peterson had the misfortune of becoming the first pilot to crash there and be killed. Peterson's accident led to the naming of the base. Many military units have used the base since its inception. The North American Aerospace Defense Command (NORAD, the folks who track Santa's travels on Christmas Eve) now has its headquarters there.

PIKE. Zebulon Pike Jr. (1779–1813) was an army brigadier general and explorer who led a trip of discovery into what is now Colorado in 1806 and 1807. Pikes Peak, a 14,115-foot Front Range mountain that ranks thirtieth on the list of Colorado's highest mountains, was named after him. (The Spanish explorers who preceded Pike in this area called the mountain El Capitán.) Pike and his men started to climb the mountain in November 1806 but turned back well before reaching the summit. Pike later wrote in his journal that he "believed no human being could have ascended to its pinical." (This was before spell check.) Grammarians debated for decades whether the name of the mountain should be Pike's Peak or Pikes Peak. Those opposing the apostrophe finally won out, but not without continuing grumbling by the losers. Pike was killed in 1813, shortly after his promotion to brigadier general, during the War of 1812. At the time of his death, Pike was leading a successful mission to capture

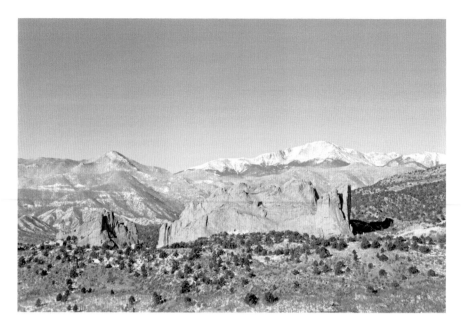

Pikes Peak—America's mountain—with the Garden of the Gods in the foreground. *Photo by author.*

Fort York, where the city of Toronto is now located. He died from falling rocks and debris after the British, on their way out the door, blew up the fort.

Platte. This name is the feminine iteration of a French adjective meaning "flat." The name was given to the Platte River (*Rivière Platte*) way back in 1739 by two French explorers, the Mallet brothers. They probably first saw the river in Nebraska and not Colorado, but in any event, they described it in a letter back home as being a mile wide and an inch deep. As an aside here, the name "Nebraska" came from two words out of the language of the Omaha Indian tribe, *ne braska*, meaning flat water. The Indian words presumably referred to the Platte River, which crosses the entire state of Nebraska.

Poudre. This is a French word (correctly pronounced *poo*-druh and routinely mispronounced *poo*-der) meaning "powder," in particular gunpowder. One theory has it that French fur trappers in the 1820s were caught in a horrific snowstorm and had to bury some of their supplies, including gunpowder, along the banks of what later became known as the Cache La Poudre River. This remains the official name of the river, although it is frequently called just the Poudre River. This river runs for 126 miles from its headwaters in Rock Mountain National Park through the city of Fort Collins and on to its confluence with the South Platte River five miles east of Greeley. A second theory about the name (which literally translates as "hide the powder") has employees of the American Fur Company burying supplies, including barrels of gunpowder, during a trek across Colorado in an effort to lighten the loads their teams would have to carry. The American Fur Company was founded in 1808 by one of America's first big-time wheeler-dealers, John Jacob Astor. In the aftermath of the American War of Independence, Astor was able to take over much of the fur trade previously controlled by French and British companies. By the 1830s, however, the demand for beaver-related clothing was (thankfully) in decline, and the American Fur Company ended up in bankruptcy in 1842. Astor had been smart enough to sell his interest some twelve years earlier.

REDCLOUD. There might have been an Indian chief named Redcloud, but this name makes it onto our list because of Redcloud Peak, a 14,043-foot mountain (forty-sixth on the list of Colorado's fifty-three fourteeners) in the San Juan Mountains in southwestern Colorado. The name was given to the mountain sometime around 1874 by the first man known to have climbed it, J.C. Spiller. Spiller was at the time the chief topographer for the U.S. Geological Survey, a position that apparently gave him naming rights for mountains. The name comes from the mountain's distinctive red color. An earlier survey team had named the mountain simply Red Mountain. Spiller embellished on that.

RIFLE. This name came about because a soldier, or possibly a trapper, accidentally left his rifle behind when the group he was with moved on to another location sometime around 1880. When he went back to get his rifle, he found it by a creek, which was thereupon named Rifle Creek. Some ten years later, the town of Rifle, which is in what became the Interstate 70 corridor along the Colorado River in west-central Colorado, was then named after the creek. There are two Colorado state parks along Rifle Creek: Rifle Gap, where there is a large reservoir, and Rifle Falls, where there is a dramatic waterfall.

SCHRIEVER. This name comes from General Bernard A. Schriever (1910–2005), known as the father of the United States Air Force's space and missile program. Schriever died in 2005 after a long and distinguished air force career. Schriever Air Force Base, originally named Falcon Air Force Base, sits just to the east of Colorado Springs and is now home to the Fiftieth Space Wing, whose mission is "commanding space and cyber systems to deliver global combat effects" and whose priorities include to "innovate space and cyber operations to stay ahead of the enemy."

SEDGWICK. This name comes from Major General John Sedgwick (1813–1864). General Sedgwick had the misfortune of being the highest-ranking officer in the Union army to be killed during the Civil War. He was taken out by a Confederate sharpshooter at the Battle of the Spotsylvania Court House. Sedgwick's connection to Colorado comes from an 1860 assignment he carried out to build a new fort along the Platte River in what is now northeast Colorado. Another fort, established nearby in 1864 in what is now Julesburg, Colorado, and originally named the Post at Julesburg Station, was renamed Fort Sedgwick in 1865. Sedgwick County, in the far northeast corner of Colorado, was formed in 1889 out of land initially a part of Logan County.

SHERMAN. This name is found in Colorado and elsewhere in recognition of the accomplishments of General William Tecumseh Sherman (1820–1891), who led the Union army to significant victories during the Civil War. General Sherman, in a speech to the graduating class of the Michigan Military Academy in 1879, is given credit for originating the famous phrase "war is hell," although this would hardly seem to have been a groundbreaking insight into human history. One of Colorado's 14,000-foot peaks, in the Mosquito Range in central Colorado just to the west of Fairplay, carries General Sherman's name. At 14,036 feet, Mount Sherman ranks forty-fifth on the list of Colorado fourteeners. A fellow Civil War general, Philip Henry Sheridan (known to his friends as "Little Phil"), also had his name assigned to a Colorado mountain. However, Mount Sheridan, which lies directly to the south of Mount Sherman, is a mere 13,748 feet.

SNOWMASS. This name comes from a large and prominent snowfield that lies in an amphitheater-like area on the eastern flank of what is now officially named Snowmass Mountain. Snowmass Mountain, at 14,092 feet, stands at number thirty-one on Colorado's list of fourteeners. The name was given to the mountain, which is in the Elk Range in west-central Colorado, by the U.S. Government Hayden Survey of 1873–75. The Ute Indians called this mountain the Cold Woman because it seemed to be the birthplace of all bad weather in the area. The mountain was also known as White House

Peak due to its proximity to Capitol Peak. Local miners sometimes called the mountain the Twins since it has two summits. Both summits are over 14,000 feet, but the lower summit doesn't get its own designation as a fourteener because it doesn't meet the "prominence" test. That is, the lower summit is connected by a saddle to the higher summit, and the elevation change between the two summits is less than 300 vertical feet.

THOMPSON. The Big Thompson River is a major Colorado river, having its headwaters in Rocky Mountain National Park. It then flows for seventy-eight miles, through the town of Estes Park and on to its confluence with the South Platte River east of Greeley. The Little Thompson River, some fifty-one miles in length, lies to the south and joins up with the Big Thompson east of Greeley, just before the Big Thompson flows into the South Platte. As for how these rivers got their names, well, no one seems to be too sure. There are two candidates for the honor: North West Company fur trader David Thompson and mountain man Philip F. Thompson. In all events, the name had been well established by 1842, when John C. Frémont traveled through the area. Big Thompson Canyon was the scene of a horrific flash flood on July 31, 1976, that claimed the lives of 143 people, 5 of whose bodies were never found.

TORREY. Torreys Peak, like nearby Grays Peak, was first climbed by botanist Charles C. Parry in 1861. As with Grays Peak, Parry named the peak after a fellow botanist, in this case John Torrey. As with Asa Gray and Grays Peak, Torrey didn't see the mountain that bore his name until many years later—in 1872, eleven years after its naming. Torreys Peak, at 14,267 feet, is the eleventh-highest mountain in Colorado.

WETTERHORN. Wetterhorn means "weather peak" in German and comes to Colorado from a mountain in south-central Switzerland with this name. Colorado's Wetterhorn Peak is in the San Juan Range in southwest Colorado and, at 14,015 feet, ranks forty-ninth on the list of Colorado's 14,000-foot peaks. On some lists, San Luis Peak, also in the San Juan Range, competes with Wetterhorn Peak for the forty-ninth spot on the list. The list I've been using, however, has San Luis Peak 1 foot lower in elevation, in fiftieth position. The name Wetterhorn was given to the mountain by Lieutenant William Marshall in 1874 while he was participating in one of the U.S. government's official mapping and surveying expedition known as the Wheeler Survey. Switzerland's Wetterhorn, although more famous, is a mere 12,153 feet.

WHEELER. This name comes from George M. Wheeler (1842–1905), a West Point graduate, explorer and cartographer who led one of the four Great Surveys. Wheeler's expedition, which started in 1872 and ended in 1879, was charged with mapping the United States west of the 100th meridian on a scale of eight inches per mile. In Colorado, Wheeler's name lives on with the Wheeler Geologic Area. This is a beautiful and dramatic outcropping of highly eroded layers of volcanic ash lying roughly ten miles east-northeast of Creede, Colorado, in Mineral County; it requires a strenuous seven-mile hike to reach. The area was Colorado's first national monument, and it held national monument status from 1908 to 1950. Now, it's a part of the La Garita Wilderness

WILSON. Although President Woodrow Wilson might get credit for some Colorado place names, when it comes to mountains, the credit goes to Allen David "A.D." Wilson (1844–1920). Wilson was one of the preeminent geographers and mountaineers of the nineteenth century. He was involved in the Hayden Survey of the western United States in 1873–75. In 1879, he became the chief topographer for the United States Geological Survey. Two of Colorado's fourteeners, Mount Wilson (at 14,246 feet, number sixteen) and Wilson Peak (at 14,017 feet, number forty-eight), both in the San Juan mountains of southwestern Colorado, bear his name. Wilson is credited with making the first recorded ascent of Mount Wilson, as well as four other Colorado fourteeners. Along with Clarence King, he was instrumental in exposing the Great Diamond Hoax of 1872, which involved the seeding of a remote area in northwest Colorado with cheap diamond fragments purchased in Europe, resulting in a frenzied Rocky Mountains diamond rush. The fraudsters, Phil Arnold and John Slack, a couple of luckless prospectors from Kentucky, sold their worthless diamond mine claims to a syndicate made up of some very sophisticated financiers from San Francisco and New York (Rothschild, Tiffany, Greeley and others) for $660,000. Neither Arnold nor Slack was ever successfully prosecuted for this crime.

ZIRKEL. This name comes from Ferdinand Zirkel, a German geologist who, in 1874, assisted Clarence King in his famous 40th parallel surveying expedition. In appreciation for his help, King gave Zirkel's name to a 12,180-foot mountain (Mount Zirkel) in northwest Colorado, on the Continental Divide between Jackson and Routt Counties. The Mount Zirkel name was then given to a federal wilderness area in Routt National Forest. I was there many years ago on a backpacking trip, and I still remember hearing the very loud and very nearby roar of a bear or a mountain lion (or possibly a Tyrannosaurus rex) that froze my dog and me in our tracks and led to a hasty retreat.

CHAPTER 4

PROSPECTORS
AND MINERS

The prospecting and mining boom-and-bust cycles that are at the heart of much of Colorado's early development had their start in 1858, when small amounts of gold were discovered in an area near present-day Denver, where Cherry Creek enters the South Platte River. Thanks to wildly exaggerated rumors about this find, what became known as the Pikes Peak gold rush began, even though the find in question was seventy-plus miles from Pikes Peak. With the California gold rush of 1849 fresh in their minds, people—the '59-ers they were called—flocked to Colorado to seek their fortune. But before the end of 1859, over a period of a mere six months, the boom had turned to bust, and the trails connecting Colorado (not yet a territory) with towns along the Missouri River were filled with eastbound disappointed and angry former prospectors—known as "go-backers"—who felt they had been duped into coming west.

Then, however, gold started to be found up in the mountains, and for some, the dream of riches derived from gold stayed alive. More importantly, perhaps, was the fact that forward-looking entrepreneurs began to realize fortunes could be made in Colorado from commerce, agriculture and real estate, giving rise to the development and eventual incorporation of Denver as a western hub of economic activity. This, in turn, led to Colorado becoming a territory in 1861, cobbled together from land taken from the New Mexico, Utah, Kansas and Nebraska Territories and, despite opposition from many sources, a state in 1876.

After the Pikes Peak gold rush flamed out, the next big mining boom-and-bust events in Colorado had to do with silver. The area around Leadville, which looked like an abandoned landfill after gold petered out in the early 1860s, came roaring back to life starting in 1877. Geologists and mining engineers came to realize that silver in great abundance was to be found here, embedded in lead carbonate rock, and that the silver could be removed from the rock using a cost-effective process of smelting. In 1878, some forty thousand people swarmed into the area, causing Leadville to adopt its name and be incorporated that same year. Although many of the people who came to Leadville left disappointed, in 1880 Leadville was still Colorado's second-largest community behind Denver with a population of some fifteen thousand. At the height of the boom, Leadville had thirty-one restaurants, thirty-five brothels, 115 gambling houses, 120 saloons and four banks.

But in 1880, as had happened with gold, the silver deposits started to play out. This was first reported at what had been one of Leadville's most productive mines: the Little Pittsburg. From late 1879 to late 1880, the value of Little Pittsburg stock went from $34.00 per share to $1.95 per share. Some of the big investors in this mine, no doubt trading on insider information, got out before the stock plummeted. Others weren't as fortunate.

Silver, however, continued to be a valuable mineral, and during the 1880s, silver mining drove the growth of several mountain towns, including Aspen, Creede, Ouray, Silverton and Telluride. Then, in the first half of the 1890s, the law of supply and demand, and changing policies coming out of Washington, resulted in a precipitous drop in the price of silver. This, coupled with a severe drought, brought hard times to all of Colorado.

Although mining continues to be an important (and still a boom and bust) industry in Colorado, the state's last big mineral rush was again based on gold and came from the discovery of gold near Cripple Creek in 1890 by a cowboy/occasional prospector named Bob Womack. Few people other than Womack thought that gold could be found in this area, but he persevered and was proven right. Womack, however, sold out his claim to the El Paso Lode early and died a poor man. On the other hand, Winfield

Opposite, middle: Eventually, gold mining needed bigger tools. Here's a mining dredge that worked the Middle Fork of the South Platte River around Fairplay, Colorado, for many years. *Park County Local History Archives*.

Opposite, bottom: Here's another big mining tool—the shovel attachment for some kind of very large mining device. *Photo by author*.

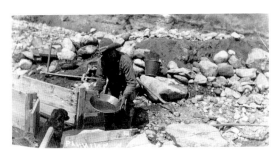

Panning for gold was a low-cost way to get into the mining business when the Colorado gold rush began. Note the attentive canine supervision here. *Park County Local History Archives.*

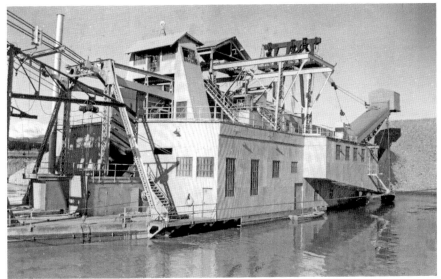

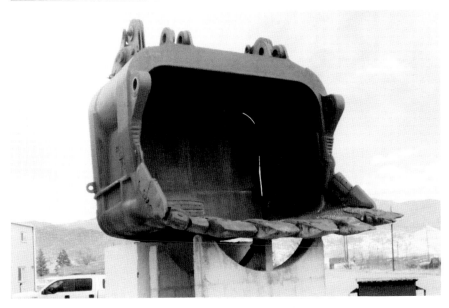

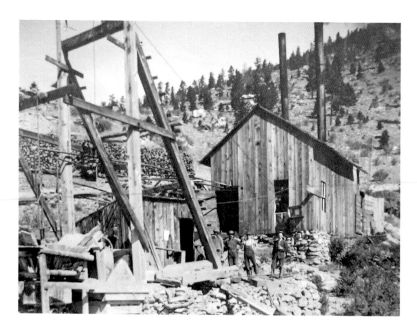

The Great Western Mine near Alma, Colorado. What would OSHA say about this? *Park County Local History Archives.*

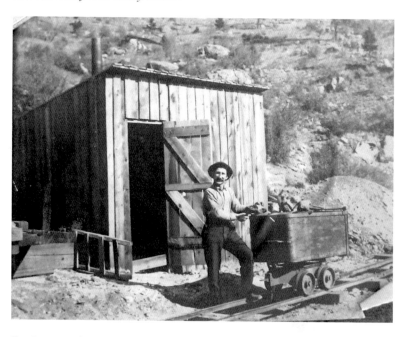

For those wanting an outdoor job and plenty of exercise, working at the Great Western Mine would have been just the thing, except perhaps in winter. *Park County Local History Archives.*

Scott Stratton, a Colorado Springs carpenter and weekend prospector, discovered the Independence Mine (on July 4, 1891, hence the name) and acquired vast wealth as a consequence. Stratton died in 1902 at the age of fifty-four. To the considerable irritation of relatives who thought he should have left more of his fortune to them, Stratton transferred the bulk of his wealth to a private foundation supporting the needs of down-and-out children and the elderly. The Cripple Creek mining boom, although compromised by violent labor conflicts, continued into the early years of the twentieth century.

As you would expect, prospecting and mining in Colorado played an important role in the naming of places. With the possible exception of the eastern plains, where mineral deposits have been few and far between, that legacy remains.

ALMA. This name, given to a mining camp on the west side of South Park in 1872, comes from a pioneer woman named Alma. However, there are three candidates for this position: Alma James, wife of a merchant who opened

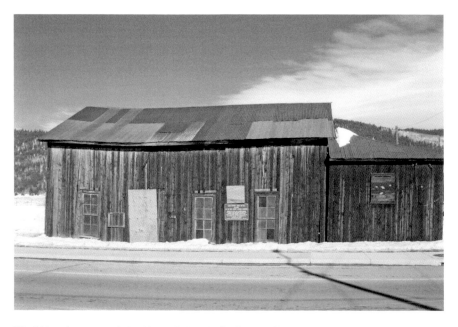

World headquarters of the Alma, Colorado Ladies Aid Society. *Photo by author.*

the first store in nearby Fairplay; Alma Graves, wife of Abner Graves, who operated the Alma Mine; and Alma Jaynes, the popular daughter of an early settler. Alma still exists as an incorporated town (and speed trap) along Colorado Highway 9 just to the north of Fairplay and to the south of Hoosier Pass. For many years, Alma had only one bar, which proudly promoted this fact in its signage. But then another bar came along and proudly promoted itself as Alma's "only other bar." Alma made national news in 1998 when a fifty-year-old part-time snow plow driver named Thomas Leask went on a rampage, shooting and killing the town's former mayor, firebombing the town hall and driving a frontend loader into the town's post office, fire department and water treatment plant. Leask, who was promptly packed away to a psychiatric hospital, was unhappy because the town was requiring him to hook up his property to the town's central water system.

ARGENTINE. This word means "silvery" or "silver like" and comes from the Latin word for silver, *argentum*. Argentine Pass runs between Summit County and Clear Creek County and is best thought of as a foot trail. The pass rises to 13,132 feet and is the highest Continental Divide crossing in the Rocky Mountains. Once upon a time, there was a mining camp known as Argentine and a mining district known as East Argentine. There is still an Argentine Peak in Clear Creek County with a summit elevation of 13,738 feet (and a ski run named argentine at the Keystone ski area).

AURARIA. This name comes to Colorado from Auraria, Georgia. In 1858, the name was given to a mining camp in what is now a part of Denver by one of the mining camp's founders, who hailed from the Georgia city. This naming was thoughtful on his part and not just a manifestation of homesickness, as *auraria* is a Latin word for "gold mine."

BROSS. This name comes from William Bross (1813–1889). Bross was the lieutenant governor of Illinois from 1865 to 1869, but he also found time to hang out in Colorado, where he acquired mining properties near the town of Alma. In 1868, Bross climbed Mount Lincoln and was so impressed by the view that he belted out a hymn, apparently heard for miles around. Rumors of this event led to what was formerly known as the south summit of Mount Lincoln getting its own name: Mount Bross. A technical rule of topography—a concept known as "prominence"—permitted (but just barely) the separate designation of this summit as one of Colorado's fourteeners. Under the prominence rule, a summit must be at least 300 feet above a saddle connecting two mountain peaks to have its own designation as a fourteener. Mount Bross, in the Mosquito Range in central Colorado, is, at 14,172 feet, the state's twenty-second-highest peak. Nearby Mount Lincoln, at 14,286 feet, sits at number eight. William Bross, a staunch Republican, might have been distressed to know that the nearest fourteener to Mount Bross, other than Mount Lincoln, is Mount Democrat. Mount Bross, however, towers over Mount Democrat by 23 feet.

BUCKSKIN JOE. This name comes from a guy named Joseph Higginbottom who always dressed in deerskin clothing, so people started calling him "Buckskin Joe." And they started calling an old mining camp where Joe hung out, and where gold was discovered in 1859, by the same name. There's now nothing left of the mining camp turned town, which was a few miles west of present-day Alma, other than a cemetery. However, the name lived on for many years in the form of a reconstructed western town theme park/tourist attraction near the Royal Gorge, not far from Cañon City. The theme park was initially built by Metro-Goldwyn-Mayer as a set for western movies, and many well-known movies were filmed there, including *Cat Ballou* (with Jane Fonda and Lee Marvin) and *The Cowboys* (with John Wayne). The only structure in the theme park that came from the original town of Buckskin Joe was the general store. In 2010, a Florida billionaire and western lore buff, William Koch, purchased Buckskin Joe and moved the buildings to his Colorado ranch, near Gunnison, for his private enjoyment.

CALUMET. *Calumet* is a French word referring to the ceremonial peace pipe used by Indians in the Rocky Mountain region. A town named Calumet sprang up in 1904 north and west of Walsenburg during the coal mining boom in this area. Calumet, like many other towns in this area whose existence tied to coal mining, is now a ghost town.

CENTRAL. Central City got its name because its location made it a hub for activity at the numerous mines active in the area during the Pikes Peak gold rush days. Central City is the county seat of Gilpin County. However, a part of it also lies in Clear Creek County (which must result in a certain amount of governmental chaos).

COAL. This name, of course, comes from the mineral. Coal has been an important resource in Colorado since before it became a state, and the word *coal* shows up all over the place. There are eighteen streams named

Coal Creek, three peaks named Coal Mountain and two towns with coal in the name: Coaldale, in Fremont County (where gypsum mining eventually became the main attraction), and Coalmont, in Jackson County. The coal deposits near Coalmont were close enough to the surface to allow for an early strip mining operation.

COFFEEPOT. Prospectors in the late 1870s, while wandering around the mountains in what is now Pitkin and Gunnison Counties trying to strike it rich, found an old coffeepot. The coffeepot had possibly been left behind by the Hayden Survey (whose participants should have known better than to litter). The finding of the coffeepot led to the naming of Coffeepot Pass (12,726 feet), which is crossed only by a foot trail. The coffeepot was reported to have still been in place in 1906, but in 1918, a forest ranger in the area said he could no longer find it. Perhaps some environmentally minded hiker finally picked it up and packed it out, not realizing its historical significance.

CREEDE. This name comes from Nicholas C. Creede (1843–1897), who, unlike most other prospectors, was highly successful in his profession. Creede's most famous strike-it-rich find—but only one of many—was the Holy Moses mine near the town that now bears his name. This mine became an investment of David H. Moffat, a (then) wealthy banker and financier from Denver. Moffat and his partners, convinced of Creede's talents as a prospector, bankrolled him to do further successful prospecting in the area. Creede came to Colorado in the early 1870s after serving seven years as an Indian scout in the U.S. Army. Following his military service, Creede returned home to Iowa to marry his sweetheart, only to discover she was already married—to one of his brothers. This, not surprisingly, created some family discord. Nicholas C. Creede was actually named William Harvey Creede at birth, but this matter of a lost girlfriend at the hands of his brother caused him to change his name. The town of Creede is the county seat of Mineral County (and about the only place in the county where you can buy gas and groceries).

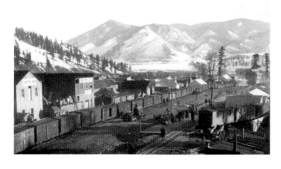

Creede, Colorado, during its mining heyday. *Colorado Springs Pioneers Museum.*

In 1889, before Nicholas Creede's discovery of the Holy Moses mine, the town's population was 600. Two years later, in 1891, it was 10,000. In the 2010 census, the town's population was measured at 290. As for Moffat, well, he spent most of his fortune in an unsuccessful attempt to build a rail line running directly west from Denver to Salt Lake City.

CUMBERLAND. Cumberland is a historic county in far northwest England, ownership of which, starting in the twelfth century, regularly changed hands between England and Scotland as a consequence of wars, revolutions, births, deaths, marriages, divorces, land swaps and so on. Cumberland Pass, in west-central Colorado, not far from the town of Gunnison, ranks fourth on the list of Colorado mountain passes crossed by an improved road, but only if you count the summit of Trail Ridge Road as a pass, which most people don't because it's too flat. If you take Trail Ridge Road off the list, Cumberland Pass moves up to number three. In any event, the summit of Cumberland Pass is 12,015 feet. (The high point along Trail Ridge Road is 12,183 feet.) Cumberland Pass connects the old mining towns of Tin Cup and Pitkin. Although the road over Cumberland Pass is not paved, it can be traveled with a standard two-wheel-drive passenger vehicle. (Shock absorber life, however, may be compromised.) It is perhaps appropriate for a pass in the Colorado mountains to be named Cumberland since the highest point in England, Scafell Pike (3,208 feet), is in Cumberland County. As an aside here, if you're looking for a restaurant in Tin Cup, you may be limited to Frenchy's Café. The original Frenchy, now long gone, was an old miner who decided he could make more money selling whiskey to other miners than prospecting for gold.

DACONO. The town of Dacono in Weld County (north-central Colorado) got its name from the first two initials of the first names of three ladies who lived there: Daisy Baum, Cora Van Horhies and Nona (or possibly Nora) Brook. The town was initially settled in 1901, and early residents were coal miners working at mines in the area. Before the town took the name Dacono, Daisy Baum's husband, Charles, gave this same name to one of the area's coal mines that he owned.

DILLON. This name comes from an early day prospector named Tom Dillon. After getting himself lost in the mountains and finally emerging in what is now Golden, Colorado, Dillon described an area he had visited before getting lost where three rivers came together. Later explorers found the area Dillon had described—with the rivers being the Blue River, the Snake River and Ten Mile Creek—and his name was eventually given to a town site at that location. The town site was moved a few times to accommodate changes in rail line locations. It was moved a final time in 1961 because of the construction of Dillon Dam and Dillon Reservoir. The 1961 relocation included moving the town cemetery, among other things. The two original Dillon town sites are now at the bottom of the reservoir, visited only by fish and scuba divers. Dillon Reservoir is a part of Denver's water supply, with the water from the reservoir transported from the west side of the Continental Divide to the South Platte River drainage on the east side of the Continental Divide by means of the Harold D. Roberts Tunnel.

Dolly Varden. This name, given to one of the more productive and longer-lasting mines located west of Alma, Colorado, comes from a minor character in a sprawling and seldom-read 1841 novel by Charles Dickens, *Barnaby Rudge*. The character whose name was given to the novel, Barnaby, is best remembered for having had a pet raven that went everywhere with him. In the 1870s, the name Dolly Varden was also given to a popular, multicolored style of dress. This, in turn, led to the name being given to a species of trout found in the Northwest United States (including Alaska) and the west coast of Canada.

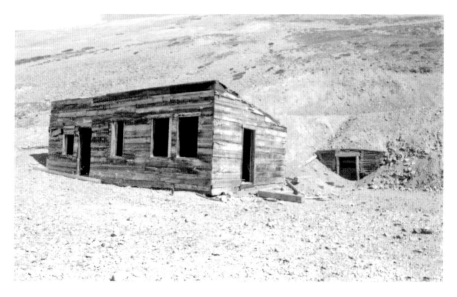

The Dolly Varden mine—one of the mines west of Alma, Colorado, that had some staying power. *Park County Local History Archives.*

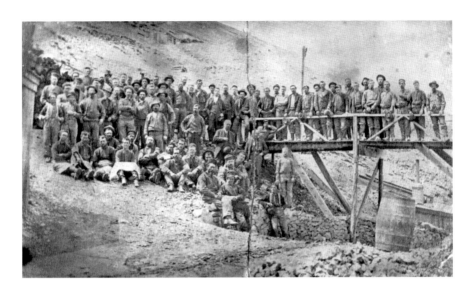

Staff meeting at the Dolly Varden mine. *Park County Local History Archives.*

ERIE. This name comes to Colorado from Erie, Pennsylvania. In 1871 or thereabouts, a local minister gave the name to a coal mining town that straddles the common border between Boulder and Weld Counties. Said minister apparently hailed from Erie, Pennsylvania, and may have been homesick. Colorado's Erie has experienced rapid growth in recent years because many Front Range places—namely, Denver, Boulder, Greeley, Fort Collins and Denver International Airport—are all within easy striking distance (assuming no major traffic debacles along the way). The name Erie originally came from an Iroquoian Indian tribe, which had a substantial presence in the area around what is now Lake Erie.

FAIRPLAY. Fairplay (originally Fair Play) began life as one of the forty-plus mining camps established in Park County after the Colorado gold rush hit its peak in 1859. Apparently, the miners who started this camp had been burned by greedy and deceitful conduct at other nearby mining camps (notably Tarryall), and they wanted this new camp to be a place where there would be, well, fair play. (Greed being what it is, whether this goal was achieved is open to doubt.) Only a few of the early Park County mining camps have survived, including, in addition to Fairplay, Alma and Como. When Fairplay was first incorporated in 1869, its name was changed to South Park City. Five years later, however, the Fairplay name was reinstated. A reasonably authentic reproduction of what Fairplay

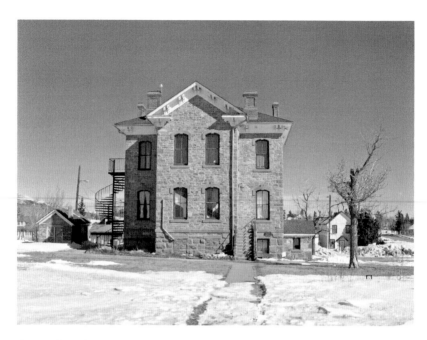

The old Park County Courthouse in Fairplay, Colorado—scene of Colorado's last legally authorized hanging. You don't want to speed in Fairplay. *Photo by author.*

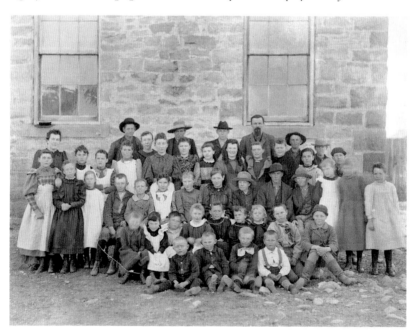

Student body and faculty at an early school in Fairplay, Colorado. *Park County Local History Archives.*

looked like in the late 1800s lives on in the form of a tourist attraction called South Park City. Fairplay is now the county seat for Park County. This status, along with tourism, provides the town with an economic base modestly more dependable than mining.

GOLDEN. This name doesn't—at least not directly—come from the metal. It comes from Thomas L. Golden, who hailed from Georgia and was one of the first prospectors to show up in Jefferson County when the Pikes Peak gold rush began. The city of Golden, founded as a mining camp in 1859, was named after him. Golden sits along Clear Creek and is home to the Colorado School of Mines, the National Earthquake Center and, most importantly, the Coors Brewing Company. Famous western showman William F. "Buffalo Bill" Cody is buried on nearby Lookout Mountain. Golden was the capital of the Colorado Territory from 1862 to 1867. The capital, for better or for worse, was then moved east twelve miles to Denver.

HUMBOLDT. This name honors the accomplishments of Friedrich Wilhelm Heinrich Alexander von Humboldt (1769–1859)—"Alex" to his friends. Humboldt was a famous German geographer, explorer, naturalist and mountaineer. However, it's unlikely he ever set foot in Colorado. In 1874, the Humboldt name was given to a highly productive silver mine on the west side of the Wet Mountain Valley in south-central Colorado. The name was then given to Humboldt Peak, which lies to the west of the mine in the Sangre de Cristo Range. Humboldt Peak, at 14,064 feet, holds position number thirty-seven on the list of Colorado's highest mountains. The Wet Mountain Valley was settled by German immigrants coming west from Chicago in 1870. They initially tried to establish a cooperative community in a town they called Colfax. However, that didn't last long. Their communal store and everything in it was, early on, destroyed by a gunpowder explosion. The town's immigrant population then spread out and took up occupancy in the Wet Mountain Valley in more traditional ways.

INDEPENDENCE. This name shows up in Colorado because a group of miners from Leadville discovered gold at a location in the upper Roaring Fork River Valley on (or about) July 4, 1879. These miners started a settlement near their strike and named it Independence since their strike had occurred on (or about) Independence Day. The name carried over to Independence Pass because the bottom of the pass, on its westerly side, is near where the strike occurred; the pass is where the miners, on the way to their discovery, had crossed over the mountains. Their crossing, it seems, was in violation of an order from Colorado's governor that settlers should stay east of the Continental Divide because land west of the divide was Ute Indian territory and no agreement had yet been reached with the Utes establishing rights to this land. Independence Pass rises to 12,095 feet and is the second-highest pass in Colorado served by a paved road. Cottonwood Pass, a bit to the south and at 12,124 feet, holds first place. However, only the road on the east side of Cottonwood Pass is paved, so perhaps Independence Pass has a claim to first place. (Trail Ridge Road, in Rocky Mountain National Park, is paved and rises to 12,183 feet. However, the point at which this occurs is not officially recognized as a pass because the road there is so flat.) Zebulon Pike is given credit for the first sighting of Independence Pass by an American explorer. Pike's sighting occurred in 1806 while he was wandering around Colorado on his mission to learn what the United States actually got for its money in the 1803 transaction with France known as the Louisiana Purchase. Independence Pass, which was originally named Hunter Pass, connects Twin Lakes on the east to Aspen on the west and is closed in winter due to heavy snow. The "Independence" name shows up again as the name of the gold mine staked out and claimed by Winfield Scott Stratton on July 4, 1891. Stratton's Independence Mine made him a rich man. Not so the miners who staked a claim on the west side of Independence Pass.

KEBLER. This name comes from Julian Abbot Kebler (1858–1903). He was an executive with Colorado Fuel & Iron Company, which had significant coal mining interests near Crested Butte. Kebler's name lives on thanks to Kebler Pass. Gunnison County Road 12 crosses over Kebler Pass, connecting Crested Butte on the east with Paonia State Park on the west, and rising to 10,007 feet along the way. The road is mostly gravel, but for some reason, small sections at the summit are paved. There is no winter maintenance. However, regular passenger vehicles can travel this road before it shuts down for the snow season. (Note: winter comes early and stays late in these parts.) Kebler Pass is in the West Elk Mountains—a nice place to enjoy the fall color display of the aspen trees.

KOKOMO. This is an Indian word meaning "young grandmother," and it came to Colorado from Kokomo, Indiana. In the late 1870s, the name was given to a silver mining boomtown at 10,695 feet in what became known as the Tenmile mining district near Leadville. Some of the miners there apparently hailed from Indiana. During the height of the silver rush, Kokomo had a population of ten thousand. After the silver ran out, the town hung on in a small way for several decades. However, the site was eventually purchased by the operators of the giant Climax molybdenum mine for use as a dumpsite for tailings. The Kokomo town site is now buried under tons of this stuff, so don't plan a visit.

LEADVILLE. This name was given to a mining boomtown in the upper Arkansas River Valley where silver was discovered in 1876 and 1877. The town had many names (including Slabtown) before the time came to adopt a final and permanent name. There was much controversy about the final naming of the town, but a local storekeeper who later became a wealthy mine investor, Horace Tabor, favored Leadville and eventually prevailed. The name chosen by Tabor came from the fact that there were large deposits of silver-bearing lead ores in the area. Leadville, now officially a city, is the county seat for Lake County.

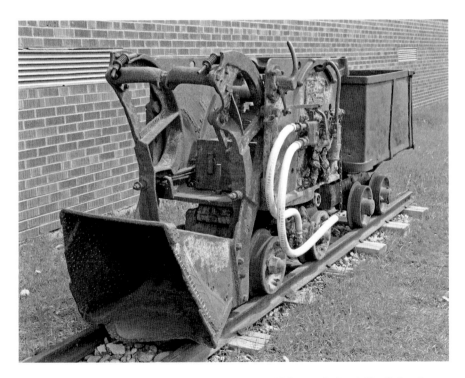

Ore car outside the National Mining Hall of Fame and Museum in Leadville, Colorado. *Photo by author.*

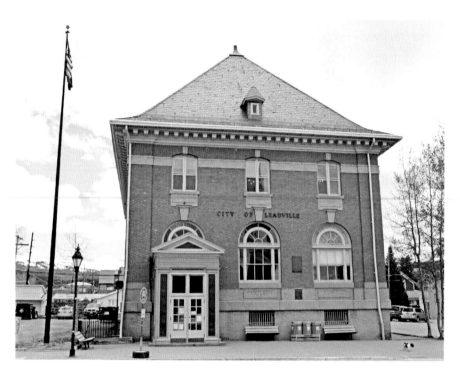

Town hall, Leadville, Colorado. *Photo by author.*

MONARCH. A mining camp in central Colorado was given the name Monarch in the mid-1800s. How the mining camp acquired this name isn't known. Perhaps the name came from the monarch butterfly, or perhaps it came from the desire of miners to live like monarchs after they struck it rich. In any event, although the mine is long gone, the name carried over to Monarch Pass, a major mountain pass connecting Salida on the east with Gunnison on the west, along U.S. Highway 50. Monarch Pass rises to 11,312 feet, placing it in fifteenth position on the list of Colorado mountain passes with an improved (asphalt or gravel) road. The current Monarch Pass is actually the third try at finding a route across this rugged area, resulting in an Old Monarch Pass and an Old Old Monarch Pass. At the summit of Monarch Pass, the Federal Aviation Administration maintains an automated weather station, useful to operators of small aircraft who shouldn't be anywhere close to there in the first place. There is also a scenic ride to the top of the mountain crossed by the pass.

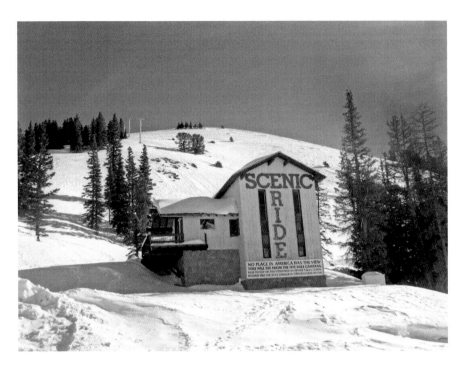

Free enterprise at work at the top of Monarch Pass. *Photo by author.*

MOSQUITO. This name, of course, comes from one of our least favorite insects. In Park County, we have the Mosquito Range mountains, Mosquito Pass, Mosquito Peak and Mosquito Creek. (Actually, there are six Mosquito Creeks in Colorado, but the best known is the one that drains easterly from the Continental Divide along the Mosquito Pass road and empties into the Middle Fork of the South Platte River between Fairplay and Alma.) These malevolent little critters are abundant in the area during the few months of the year when the temperature doesn't drop below freezing every night. There are multiple versions of the story as to how the mosquito name came to be assigned to these various places, but they generally go like this: A meeting was being held in 1861 after gold was discovered in the area for the purpose of establishing a mining district and a town. The participants at this meeting couldn't agree on a name, so they left a blank for the name in the book they were using to record their proceedings. When they got back together again a short time later and opened the book, there was a dead mosquito squashed on the page where the blank had been left for a name. The attendees at the meeting then agreed to use the name "Mosquito" for the district and the town, and use of the name for other places followed.

The road (if you can call it that) over Mosquito Pass (13,185 feet) is now a four-wheel-drive-only affair, but there was once a wagon-accessible toll road across the pass, connecting Fairplay and Leadville. Importantly, Mosquito Pass is also the location of the annual World Championship Pack Burro Race. You can find entry instructions at www.burrodays.com.

NEDERLAND. Nederland is the name in the Dutch language of the country we sometimes (incorrectly) call Holland but is officially the Kingdom of the Netherlands. The name came to be assigned to a town seventeen miles southwest of Boulder in 1874, shortly after the Nederland Mining Company, a Dutch enterprise, bought the Caribou silver mine and moved its milling operations to where the town of Nederland now sits (and where the weather was modestly better). The town site was first occupied in the 1850s as a location for trading activity between the Ute Indians in the area and European settlers. (This was before they started killing one another). Prior to its incorporation under the name Nederland, the town had several other names, including Dayton, Brown's Crossing, Brownsville, Tungsten Town and Middle Boulder. Nederland, in the Dutch language, means "low country," appropriate for Holland, much of which is below sea level. Nederland, Colorado, on the other hand, sits at 8,200 feet above sea level.

NEW CASTLE. This name comes from Newcastle, England, a famous old-world mining region. The name was given to a town along the Colorado River in northwest Colorado (Garfield County) in the 1880s after coal was discovered in the area. At the time of its founding, in the 1860s, the town was called Grand Butte for a year or so and then Chapman.

OFFICER. This name comes from James Officer, an early day miner in and around an area now known as Officer's Gulch. Officer also owned a lumber mill in the area that produced lumber products for local mines. Officer's Gulch is east of Copper Mountain and west of Frisco, along the I-70 corridor connecting these locations.

OPHIR. This name comes from the Old Testament (1 Kings 9:28). There, Ophir was the location of King Solomon's mines from which 420 talents of gold were produced and delivered to the king. (I'm sure you already knew this, but just in case you didn't, a "talent" is a measure of weight and money used in ancient Greece, Rome and the Middle East, and 420 talents was a lot of gold.) The Ophir name was given to a mining boomtown, two mountains and a mountain pass, all in San Miguel County, in far southwest Colorado. The town still exists, but a boomtown it is not.

QUANDARY. Quandary Peak, at 14,265 feet, is Colorado's thirteenth-tallest mountain. It was named by a group of miners who, in the early 1860s, came upon a mineral deposit on its slopes they could not identify. Thus, they were in a quandary over this mineral, and that led to the naming of the mountain. It's not known if they ever did figure out what the mystery mineral was— or what they were drinking when they came up with this name. Quandary Peak is in central Colorado and is a part of what is known as the Ten Mile Range. It lies some seven miles to the south of Breckenridge and presents a spectacular vista when traveling south on Colorado Highway 9 from Breckenridge toward Hoosier Pass.

RALSTON. Lewis Ralston, a prospector from Georgia on his way to the gold fields of California, is given credit for the first discovery of gold in Colorado, although a French trapper, Eustace Carrière, may deserve the honor. Carrière apparently found small quantities of gold in what is now Colorado in 1835. He took his findings back to New Mexico, where the material was confirmed to be gold. Carrière then went back to Colorado but couldn't locate the place where he had found the deposit. Ralston's discovery took place fifteen years later, in June 1850, at a creek in central Colorado now named Ralston Creek. Ralston Creek has its headwaters in northeast Gilpin County and flows easterly thirty-two miles to Arvada, where what's left of it after irrigation withdrawals empties into Clear Creek. Ralston's discovery didn't seem to create much excitement since California continued to be the prospecting hot spot in 1850. The Colorado gold rush didn't get going until nine years later, in 1859.

SCHOFIELD. This name comes from B.F. Schofield, a silver miner who lived in what is now Gunnison County in the 1870s and 1880s. He may also have been a judge, or at least he called himself a judge. In all events, he founded a mining town in 1879 and gave it his name. By 1885, a mere six years later, the mining boom in this area was over, and the town was abandoned, joining the ranks of Colorado's many ghost towns. B.F. Schofield's name lives on with Schofield Pass. This pass (summit elevation of 10,722 feet) is crossed by a road called Gothic Road, which is passenger car compatible on the east (Crested Butte) side but becomes a serious 4x4 trail (going through, among other places, Devil's Punchbowl Canyon) on the west (Marble) side. Schofield Pass has at least twelve reported motor vehicle fatalities as part of its legacy.

Silverheels. This name comes from a woman who danced in the saloons of Park County during the gold rush days and whose shoes had silver heels. She became a heroine when she served as a nurse during an 1861 smallpox epidemic in and around the Buckskin Joe mining camp. The legend of Silverheels has it that she contracted the disease and quietly left the area because it had robbed her of her beauty. Mount Silverheels, a beautiful 13,817-foot peak just outside Fairplay, was named for her.

Tarryall. Tarryall was the name given to one of the first of forty-some mining camps that sprang up pretty much overnight in what is now Park County during the 1859 Colorado gold rush. The name evolved from the notion, expressed by someone, that because gold was so plentiful in the area, it was a good place for anyone and everyone to come and stay (to tarry). This, however, proved to be overly optimistic. Latecomers to Tarryall found that the gold was all gone, and the camp soon vanished, but not before it developed a reputation for greed and deceitful conduct. (The bad reputation of Tarryall led to a nearby mining camp, which was trying to do better, taking the name Fair Play, now Fairplay.) The Tarryall name lives on with Tarryall Creek, Tarryall Reservoir and the Tarryall Reservoir State Wildlife Area, all in Park County. Another small Park County town, originally named Puma City, took over the Tarryall name in the late 1800s and early 1900s. There are still a few structures and residents at this location, which lies along Tarryall Creek to the south and east of the reservoir.

Taylor. In Gunnison County, Taylor Park and the Taylor River (which in turn forms Taylor Reservoir) are named for Jim Taylor, a miner who arrived in this neck of the woods around 1860. There is also a Taylor Peak (13,153 feet) in Rocky Mountain National Park, named for an educator from Kansas who visited that area in 1895 and apparently made enough of an impression on the locals to have a mountain named after him. The Taylor River grows some really big trout in the tail water below the reservoir, but these fish are wise to the ways of fishermen and careful about what they eat.

Telluride. Telluride is a mineral containing tellurium. Tellurium is a rare chemical element (for purists, atomic no. 52/symbol Te) used in the manufacture of various metal products. Apparently, some of the gold discovered in parts of Colorado was mixed in with telluride and came to be known as "telluride gold." This, in turn, led to the naming of a mining camp turned town in southwest Colorado, although telluride gold was not actually present in this area. The town, founded in 1878, was originally named Columbia, but that resulted in confusion with a California town by the same name, so the name was changed. Telluride, along the San Miguel River, is the county seat for San Miguel County, and it is now home to a big-time upscale ski resort (with, as expected, big-time real estate prices).

TINCUP. There are various theories as to how the name Tincup came to be given to a mining town in Gunnison County originally called Virginia City. One such theory has it that ore samples at the local assay office were weighed in tin cups. Another is that some of the local miners used tin cups to pan for gold. In all events, this was a booming place in the 1880s and 1890s, as well as a violent place, with two town marshals having been shot to death during this time. There's not much left of Tincup now other than the Tincup Store and Frenchy's Café. Nonetheless, it remains a popular tourist stop not far from Taylor Reservoir. If you visit, don't expect your cellphone to work.

VICTOR. This name, given to a mining camp in Teller County not far from better-known Cripple Creek, came from an early settler in the area, Victor Adams. Adams's family has reported that when the time came to name the community, several names were placed in a hat, and Victor was the name drawn. Victor was founded in 1891 after gold was discovered in the area. The settlement went from nonexistent to a population of 18,000 by the turn of the century. However, after the ore largely ran out, violent labor disputes erupted and a large number of the miners left to fight World War I and never came back, the population plunged just as rapidly. The 2010 census reported Victor's population at 397. During the boom times, Victor became known as the "City of Mines," and it still calls itself the "City of Gold Mines." Despite its modest size, Victor was incorporated as a city and not a town, and it retains that official designation.

WEBSTER. In 1878, the Webster brothers, William and Emerson, decided they could make some money operating a toll road connecting Park and Summit Counties. Their toll road, in the general vicinity of the current Keystone Resort, crossed the Continental Divide and gave access to an area where prospectors were in hot pursuit of the next big find. What remains of the Webster brothers' entrepreneurial exercise is a jeep road across what is now known as Webster Pass. This road tops out at 12,103 feet and is not for the faint of heart. Crossing Webster Pass is reputed to be a serious 4x4 adventure, challenging to both man and machine and capable of bringing a quick end to both.

CHAPTER 5

THE RAILROADS

The construction and operation of railroads probably did more to cause Colorado to grow and prosper than anything else—even more than the discovery of gold and silver. Railroads made Colorado easily accessible for the first time to prospectors, settlers, speculators, investors, laborers, tourists, gamblers, ladies of the night and more. The railroads allowed mining and agricultural businesses to operate profitably where they could not before.

The impact of railroads in Colorado began in earnest around 1870, when the population of what was then the Colorado Territory was a tick under 40,000. In large part because of the railroads, by 1880, the population of Colorado—by then a state—exceeded 194,000.

Although building rail lines, especially through the mountains, required huge amounts of capital, labor and engineering genius, the competition for these lines was intense, resulting in much wheeling and dealing, influence peddling, questionable stock sales and, in a few instances, violence. Further in that regard, the Atchison, Topeka and Santa Fe Railway and the Denver and Rio Grande Railway came close to an armed conflict over rights to build a rail line across Raton Pass. However, when the Atchison, Topeka and Santa Fe put together a mercenary band of big-league gunslingers, including Bat Masterson and Doc Holliday, the Denver and Rio Grande backed off. But then, shortly thereafter, armed conflict did take place between the two railroads. This time, the prize was a rail line along the Arkansas River from Pueblo to

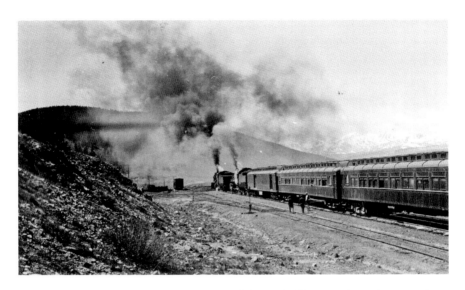

Trains played a huge role in the development of Colorado. However, the environmental movement was not well organized during the early decades of railroading in the state. *Colorado Springs Pioneers Museum.*

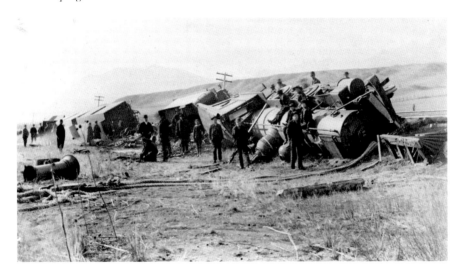

Although trains may have been safer than covered wagons, stagecoaches and ox carts, they were not immune from mishap. *Colorado Springs Pioneers Museum.*

Leadville. After a U.S. Supreme Court ruling in its favor, the Denver and Rio Grande, on June 11, 1879, removed Atchison, Topeka and Santa Fe employees from the Pueblo–Leadville rail line at gunpoint, and brief gun battles followed at several locations.

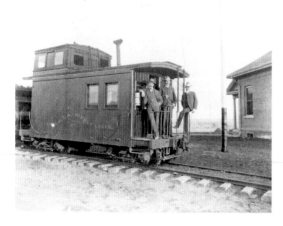

Left: Hanging out on the caboose in natty attire was apparently a popular guy thing. *Colorado Springs Pioneers Museum.*

Below: It took some sturdy four-legged critters to build railroads through the mountains of Colorado. Here, near Fairplay, is Bill McKee and his track-laying crew, along with one of their burros. *Park County Local History Archives.*

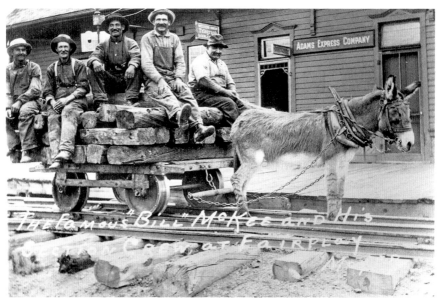

The list of railroad companies playing an important role in the development of Colorado is long. In addition to the already mentioned Atchison, Topeka and Santa Fe Railway and the Denver and Rio Grande Railway, the list includes at least the following: the Colorado Central Railroad; Kansas Pacific Railroad; Union Pacific Railroad; Chicago, Burlington and Quincy Railroad; Denver, South Park and Pacific Railroad; Burlington Railroad; Rock Island Railroad; Colorado and Southern Railroad; Denver and Rio Grande Western Railroad; Denver Pacific Railroad;

Right: Colorado towns were proud of their train depots. This one was in Colorado Springs, where General William Palmer wanted nothing but the best for his Denver and Rio Grande Railway. *Colorado Springs Pioneers Museum.*

Below: Before we had trains, we had this. *Park County Local History Archives.*

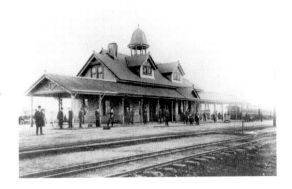

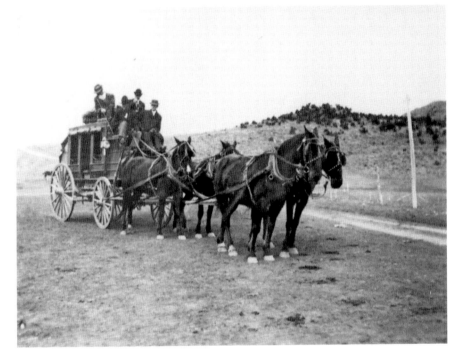

Denver and Northwestern Railroad; Rio Grande Southern Railroad; and the Colorado Midland Railway. In the mix were both lines with narrow-gauge tracks (3 foot, 0 inch) and lines with full-width tracks (4 foot, 8.5 inch).

As these railroad companies went about the business of laying tracks, they established depots and started towns and gave them names. Those names have lived on as a part of modern-day Colorado, which is not the case for most of the railroads. Through business failures and mergers and acquisitions, the list of historically significant railroads still serving Colorado is a short one. The legacy of the Atchison, Topeka and Santa Fe survives under the corporate structure of BNSF, and the legacy of the Denver and Rio Grande survives under the corporate structure of Union Pacific.

———◆———

AKRON. This name comes to Colorado by way of Akron, Ohio. In 1882 or thereabouts, the name was given to a town in northeast Colorado (Washington County) by the wife of a railroad official involved in the creation of the town. Said wife apparently came to Colorado from Akron, Ohio, and wanted her hometown name to accompany her to her new state. She might also have had in mind the fact that *akron* is a Greek word meaning "summit," and although the town of Akron is out in the eastern plains of Colorado far from the mountains, it was nonetheless, at 4,659 feet in elevation, the highest point along the Chicago, Burlington and Quincy line.

BARR. This name comes from a civil engineer with the Chicago, Burlington and Quincy Railroad. That railroad laid tracks through central Colorado in the early 1860s. We now have Barr Lake and Barr Lake State Park, in Adams County near the city of Brighton, named after him. Among other attributes, Barr Lake State Park serves as headquarters for the Rocky Mountain Bird Observatory, and bald eagles, along with numerous other migratory species, have found the park a pleasant place to spend the winter. Barr Lake's water comes from an old irrigation ditch with very senior water rights, which takes water from the South Platte River.

BOREAS. Boreas was the Greek god of the north wind and the bringer of winter. In Greek mythology, he is described as being very strong and, appropriate for someone with his job description, having a bad temper. Boreas Pass, like Hoosier Pass a bit farther to the west, connects South Park on the south with the Lake Dillon/Breckenridge area on the north. The pass tops out at 11,481 feet, placing it tenth on the list of Colorado mountain passes having an improved road (in this case a gravel road). Boreas Pass was an important route for miners during the gold rush days and was formerly traversed by a railroad line. The railroad line was abandoned in the 1930s. The Boreas name was given to the pass by Sidney Dillon, a man who was significantly involved in building railroad lines in the West, primarily for the

Union Pacific Railroad. Prior to Dillon naming the pass Boreas Pass, it was known as Breckinridge Pass. (Note the spelling here; also, find the entry for Breckenridge to learn why Breckinridge became Breckenridge.)

CALHAN. This name, given to a town in eastern El Paso County in 1888, came from Michael Calahan, who had a contract to lay tracks for the Chicago, Rock Island and Pacific Railroad from the Colorado/Kansas border to Colorado Springs. The middle *a* in Calahan's name, either by intent or mistake, was deleted when a post office for the town was applied for. The *raison d'être* for this town was as a watering station for the railroad. These were the days of steam locomotives, so water was essential to train operation. Although Calhan is thirty-five miles east of Colorado Springs, out in the plains of Colorado—which generally slope downward on their way to Kansas and Nebraska—Calhan, at 6,535 feet, is actually higher in elevation than Colorado Springs, at 6,035 feet. Thus, by the time a steam engine made it to Calhan, it was in need of water. As for the Chicago, Rock Island and Pacific Railroad, it finally shut down on March 31, 1980, after surviving more than four decades of turmoil in the railroad industry.

CLIMAX. This name came into being when, in 1884, the construction of a railroad line by the Denver, South Park and Pacific Railroad leading to Leadville made it across the summit of Fremont Pass. This was apparently the climactic moment for the track laying project, hence the name given to the station at the top of the pass. When molybdenum became a valuable mineral in the early twentieth century, the Climax Molybdenum Company was formed and began development of the Climax Mine. Thanks to the whims of the market for molybdenum, the mine, a huge open-pit operation, experienced shutdowns from 1919 to 1924 and again from 1995 to 2012, thereby serving to perpetuate the tradition of boom and bust that has been a part of Leadville since its beginning in 1859.

COLLBRAN. This name comes from Henry Collbran, a railroad executive with the Colorado Midland Railway. That railroad was active in western Colorado in the 1880s, laying tracks to service a then booming mining and agricultural industry. Henry Collbran proposed changing the name of an existing town, De Beque, to Collbran. However, the founder and namesake of that town, Dr. Wallace A.E. de Beque, objected, leading to a spirited debate and a bizarre political compromise whereby the residents of the nearby town of Hawxhurst (thirty-five miles to the southeast of De Beque) agreed to change the name of their town to Collbran. This seemed to satisfy Henry and allowed the town of De Beque to retain its name. These two towns continue their peaceful coexistence in Mesa County, to the east of Grand Junction.

DOTSERO. Although it's been suggested by some that this name, given to a small town in Eagle County along the I-70 corridor, comes from a word in the Ute language meaning "something unique," the better theory is that the name came from a start-of-the-line marking on an old Denver and Rio Grande Western Railroad map: ".0" (that is, "dot-zero"). In any event, the town sits at the base of Colorado's most recently active volcano, the Dotsero Crater, which last erupted some 4,100 years ago and is showing no signs of a repeat performance.

EADS. This name comes from James B. Eads (1820–1887), a structural engineer most famous for the construction of the Eads Bridge, which crosses the Mississippi River in St. Louis. Eads was working for the Missouri Pacific Railroad in east-central Colorado in the late 1880s when a town along the rail line was given his name. Eads is the county seat for Kiowa County. A settlement named Dayton was started near present-day Eads in anticipation of the railroad coming to the area, but then the rail line ended up three miles to the south. So, all of the buildings in Dayton were packed up and moved to the rail line location, and the name of the settlement was changed to Eads.

FRISCO. Contrary to popular belief, this name did not simply come from the city of San Francisco. It came from a railroad, the St. Louis–San Francisco Railway Company, which was sometimes referred to as the Frisco Line, using letters plucked out of its full name. In 1875, a man by the name of Captain Henry Leamed, who was affiliated with this railroad, chose a site for a depot where the town of Frisco is now located. The depot was to be constructed when the Frisco Line finally made it to Colorado. To mark the site for the anticipated new depot, Leamed tacked a sign on the cabin of one of the town's first settlers, Henry Recen, that read, "Frisco City," and the name, with "City" later dropped, stuck. As a small irony here, the Frisco Line never made it to Frisco, Colorado. Instead, it went south from its origins in Missouri along a route that took it to Frisco, Texas. Colorado's Frisco was a boomtown during the gold rush days, but then mining died out and along came the Depression. By 1930, the town's population was down to eighteen. Now, however, Frisco happily thrives due to its proximity to four world-class ski venues: Breckenridge, Copper Mountain, Keystone and Vail. Make that five, if you include Arapahoe Basin. Frisco is in Summit County, the heart of Ski Country USA.

GREENWOOD. In 1870, while Colorado was still a territory, Greenwood County was established to the south and east of Denver and named after William Greenwood, the then chief engineer of the Kansas Pacific Railway. Four years later, however, the Colorado territorial legislature did another of its many county reshuffles, and Greenwood County disappeared, with part of it going to Elbert County and the rest to Bent County. Greenwood Village, an upscale city carved out of southwest Denver in 1950, took its name from a large historic ranch in the area, the Greenwood Ranch. The ranch may have been named after Chief Engineer Greenwood, but I haven't been able to confirm that connection.

HAGERMAN. There are a couple of Hagermans making the list of Colorado names. James J. Hagerman started and ran the Colorado Midland Railway, one of the pioneering railroad companies that, in the last quarter of the nineteenth century, took on the challenge of laying tracks across inhospitable Colorado mountain terrain. This activity included the construction of a tunnel at the top of an 11,925-foot pass now known as Hagerman Pass. This pass lies to the west of Leadville, in Lake and Pitkin Counties. The railroad abandoned this route for a more direct one a few years later, but a rough-and-tumble jeep road—better for mountain bikes and pedestrians than motor vehicles—still crosses the pass. Perhaps because of misadventures such as this, the Colorado Midland Railway ended up in bankruptcy in 1897. The other Hagerman on our list is Percy Hagerman, an Aspen businessman and mountaineer credited with some of the first climbs of peaks in and around Aspen, in the Elk Range mountains. Hagerman Peak, at 13,841 feet, in the vicinity of Maroon Bells and Snowmass Mountain, was named after Percy.

HARTMAN. This name comes from George Hartman, a superintendent with the Santa Fe Railway. In the early 1900s, a town along the Santa Fe line in far southeastern Colorado (Prowers County) was named after Hartman. This naming, however, was a mistake, made in the railroad's Chicago offices. The town was supposed to be named Bristol, after C.H. Bristol, another railroad executive. To make things right with Mr. Bristol, his name was given to a different town in Prowers County. Back in the 1920s and 1930s, Hartman was a bustling place with a large sugar beet factory and grain coop, a busy railroad operation and a population in excess of five thousand. In the 1940s, however, the population began to decline. Per the 2010 census, the population of Hartman was eighty-one. Bristol has fared no better, losing its post office in 1997.

LIMON. This name comes from John Limon, who was a construction superintendent for the Chicago, Rock Island and Pacific Railroad as it worked its way across eastern Colorado in the 1880s. The town of Limon, an important highway and railroad junction in Lincoln County some seventy miles north and east of Colorado Springs, was named for him. Interstate 70, U.S. Highway 24, U.S. Highway 40 and Colorado Highway 71 all pass through Limon. Among other attributes of note, Limon seems to be ground zero for severe weather—including tornados—rolling across the plains of eastern Colorado.

MINTURN. This name comes from Thomas Minturn, another railroad man (the Denver and Rio Grande Western Railroad) whose name was given to a town along the railroad's tracks. Minturn, in Eagle County, is surrounded on three sides by the Holy Cross Wilderness. Also, the Eagle River runs through the town, and the Beaver Creek and Vail ski areas are a short drive away. Because of these amenities, Minturn is a regular stop for visitors to Colorado.

PAOLI. This name comes to Colorado thanks to General Pasquale di Paoli, a patriotic figure in the history of the much fought-over and now French-controlled Mediterranean island of Corsica. Di Paoli lived from 1725 to 1807 and was involved in numerous wars and matters of political intrigue affecting the island. This regularly resulted in his being exiled. Someone, a long time ago, named a town in Pennsylvania after Paoli, and in 1895, the chief engineer for the Chicago, Burlington and Quincy Railroad named a town after him (or after the Pennsylvania town named after him) in far northeastern Colorado. Paoli is in Phillips County (pretty much a suburb of Nebraska); but for the railroad having passed through there during the great western migration, it would probably not exist.

PHILLIPS. This name comes from R.O. (Rollo) Phillips, who was the secretary of the Lincoln Land Company. The Lincoln Land Company was chartered in 1880 by the Burlington and Missouri River Railroad, which needed to sell land given to it by the U.S. government in order to pay for the construction of its rail lines. Phillips, as part of his corporate duties, was responsible for organizing numerous towns in southwest Nebraska and northeast Colorado. Phillips County, in far northeast Colorado (a place indistinguishable from southwest Nebraska), was formed in 1889 out of land originally a part of Logan County. Phillips County describes itself, proudly, as consisting of "undulating sand hills covered with buffalo grass."

RIDGWAY. This name comes from Robert M. Ridgway, a superintendent with the Denver and Rio Grande Railway and its affiliate, the Rio Grande Southern Railroad. Ridgway had significant responsibility for the construction and operation of rail service in western Colorado intended to meet the needs of the mining industry. The town of Ridgway, in Ouray County some eighty-five miles south of Grand Junction, was founded in 1891 by the railroad and given Ridgway's name. The Rio Grande Southern's rail lines to the silver mining boomtowns of Rico and Telluride were completed just in time for the silver panic of 1893. This resulted in the shutdown of most of the silver mines in the area and loss of the revenue the railroad was counting on to recoup its investment. The railroad nonetheless struggled on, finally going out of business in 1951. The classic John Wayne western *True Grit* was filmed in this area. Also of note, Ridgway has claimed it has the only traffic light in Ouray County.

SIMLA. This name comes from a town in India where the British empire once had its summer administrative headquarters (before Mahatma Gandhi convinced the British to get out of India). The name was given to a town in Elbert County, some forty miles northeast of Colorado Springs, by a Rock Island Railroad official whose daughter was, at the time, reading a book that referenced Simla, India. She suggested Simla as the name of this town, and her father went along with the idea. Simla was first settled in 1888 and finally got around to incorporation in 1912. At one time, it was a central shipping point for potatoes grown in the area.

SPINNEY. This name comes from B.F. Spinney, who arranged train trips from Colorado Springs into the mountains on the old Colorado Midland Railway for people wanting to see and pick wildflowers. These trips became known as the "flower train." They ended when the railroad went out of business in the aftermath of World War I. However, the Leadville Colorado and Southern Railroad has kept the flower train tradition alive, with wildflower-focused excursions out of Leadville each summer. (Per the railroad's management, well-behaved pets are welcome on these trips.) Spinney's name lives on

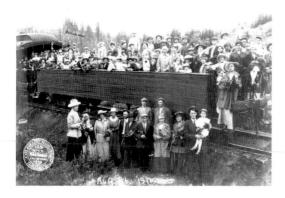

Right: Well-dressed participants on a wild flower train excursion west of Colorado Springs, organized by B.F. Spinney and with transportation provided by the long-defunct Colorado Midland Railway. *Colorado Springs Pioneers Museum.*

with Spinney Mountain State Park and Spinney Mountain Reservoir, both in South Park, in Park County. The reservoir is home to some really big rainbow trout and some really mean-looking northern pike.

STRASBURG. This name comes from John Strasburg, a section foreman for the Kansas Pacific Railroad. The small town of Strasburg, along the I-70 corridor east of Denver, was named after him. The town of Strasburg, formerly known as Comanche Crossing, claims to be the true location of the first transcontinental railroad's completion. That's because when the Golden Spike was driven at Promontory Point, Utah, on May 10, 1869, joining tracks of the Union Pacific and Central Pacific Railroads, the Union Pacific had no bridge across the Missouri River. Union Pacific passengers had to exit the train they were on and cross the river between Omaha and Council Bluffs by ferry and then get back on a train. The Kansas Pacific Railroad, on the other hand, managed to complete a bridge across the river at Kansas City before the Union Pacific completed its bridge at Omaha. This led to a meeting of track-laying crews of the Kansas Pacific Railroad at Comanche Crossing (now Strasburg) on August 15, 1870, allowing someone, for the first time, to cross the entire continent without getting off the train. History has generally ignored Strasburg's position on this first-to-complete issue and sided with Utah.

WELLINGTON. This name comes from C.L. Wellington, who was a traffic manager for the Colorado and Southern Railroad. That modest position was enough to cause his name to be given to a town in north-central Colorado (Larimer County) founded in 1902, not far from the Colorado/Wyoming border. Wellington is now bisected by I-25 and is best known as the childhood home of former Supreme Court justice Byron White, who regularly returned there for high school class reunions. The town is also remembered as the site of a wooly mammoth discovery in 2000. Unfortunately, important parts of the wooly mammoth's remains didn't survive excavation and transportation. The parts that did survive are now in the possession of the University of Colorado. Wellington has several interesting street names capturing the spirit of the Old West, such as Thundering Herd Way, Stampede Drive and Firewater Lane. Wooly Mammoth Circle marks the location of the wooly mammoth discovery. Wellington was well known as a place where, during Prohibition, travelers moving between Cheyenne and Fort Collins could stop for gas—and find a drink.

WESTCLIFFE. This name comes from Westcliff-on-the-Sea, England, the birthplace of Dr. William A. Bell. Bell was General William Palmer's business partner in many Colorado-related ventures, including the Denver and Rio Grande Railway. The town of Westcliffe got going in 1881 when the D&RG came to this part of Colorado, and Dr. Bell named the town for his old-world birthplace. Westcliffe sits in a beautiful valley between the Wet Mountains on the east and the Sangre de Cristo Range on the west. Although far removed from useful things like hospitals and shopping malls, Westcliffe, the county seat for Custer County (and pretty much all there is in Custer County), is now a venue for upscale second homes and a thriving art community. Going back a few decades, there was a nice little ski area west of town called Conquistador, which was a great place for a low-budget family ski outing. But its location was not good for snow retention, and it is no more.

CHAPTER 6

POLITICIANS, ENTREPRENEURS AND PROMOTERS

The naming of places in Colorado was greatly influenced during the last third of the nineteenth century and the early years of the twentieth century by a number of colorful entrepreneurs who acquired wealth from mining, railroads, banking, agriculture and other business activities; promoted Colorado to others as a means by which to enhance their wealth; sometimes used their wealth to attain high political office; and sometimes used high political office to further promote Colorado and thereby further enhance their wealth.

During this time, the establishment of a regulatory environment friendly to business had a higher priority than anything else. Although efforts were made to promote education; aid the poor, sick and downtrodden; and provide justice for the accused, these were subordinate to no-holds-barred wheeling and dealing. Symbolic of this was an 1888 lynching in Greeley. In that year, vigilantes broke into the Weld County Jail and hanged a man named William D. French. Of greater concern to the vigilantes than French's guilt or innocence was the fact that his arrest, incarceration and court proceedings had already cost the taxpayers of the county some $12,000. Lynchings, it seems, were thought of as a way to make government more efficient. Between 1859 and 1919, more than 170 lynchings were reported to have occurred in Colorado.

Worthy of special mention on a list of entrepreneurs/promoters/politicians leaving their mark on Colorado during its formative years would be John Evans, William Larimer, Frederick Pitkin, John Routt, David Moffat, Horace Tabor, Jerome Chaffee, Alva Adams, Mahlon Thatcher, William Jackson Palmer, John C. Osgood, John D. Rockefeller, Horace Greeley and Charles Boettcher. Many intriguing stories come from this era of free enterprise let loose to pursue its unregulated end. David Moffat, for example, once one of the wealthiest men in Colorado thanks to highly profitable and well-timed mining investments, died bankrupt and alone in a New York City hotel room in 1911 after failing to obtain East Coast financing to complete his Denver, Northwestern and Pacific Railroad. Along Moffat's path to ruin, he gutted the First National Bank of Denver, whose resources he, as an executive officer of the bank, had used to support his failed railroad. The Thatcher brothers, Mahlon and John, had to use their personal wealth to save the bank from a disastrous liquidation.

And then there was Horace Tabor, who, while a Leadville storekeeper, made some timely mine investments resulting in great wealth. Tabor, fortune in hand, moved back to Denver, divorced his dutiful wife, Augusta, and married his much younger (by twenty-four years) mistress, Elizabeth "Baby Doe" McCourt. Tabor served as lieutenant governor of Colorado for six years and as a U.S. senator for a brief period of time following the resignation of Henry Teller, who had accepted an appointment as the secretary of the interior. Tabor was a prominent philanthropist during the good times, but he lost his fortune when the price of silver collapsed in 1893. He spent the last year of his life as Denver's postmaster, no doubt an act of charity from well-connected friends.

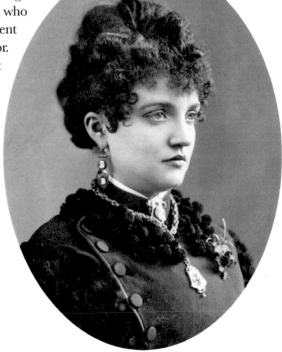

Baby Doe Tabor (aka Elizabeth McCourt). *Wikimedia Commons.*

There was also William Jackson Palmer, who used his wealth from railroads, coal, manufacturing and real estate to found the city of Colorado Springs in 1871 and, in 1874, the Colorado College—to this day Colorado's most prestigious institution of higher education. Palmer managed to preserve enough of his wealth to build a spectacular home, Glen Eyrie, just to the north of the Garden of the Gods in Colorado Springs. However, he spent the last three years of his life in a wheelchair and with chronic pain due to a 1903 equestrian accident that resulted in a broken spine.

The legacy of Colorado's politicians, entrepreneurs and promoters—a mix of good acts and bad, fortunes made and fortunes lost, personal triumphs and devastating tragedies—lives on in the form of this state's place names.

———•———

ADAMS. This name, as used in Colorado, comes from Alva Adams (1850–1922) and not John Quincy Adams, sixth president of the United States. Alva was the governor of Colorado on three separate occasions (he apparently liked the job), serving as the state's fifth (1887–89), tenth (1897–99) and fourteenth (briefly, in 1905) chief executive officer. Alva had a younger brother, William "Billy" Adams, who was Colorado's governor from 1927 to 1933, after Alva's death. Alva also had a son, Alva Blanchard Adams, who served as a U.S. senator from Colorado on two occasions, from 1923 to 1925 and again from 1933 to 1941. Adams County, part of the sprawling Denver urban complex on its north and east side, was named after Alva in 1902, when the county was formed out of land taken from Arapahoe County. In 1989, Adams County gave up fifty-three square miles of its land to the City and County of Denver for use in the construction of Denver International Airport. Adams County lost another small chunk of land in 2001 when the City and County of Broomfield came into being. One other Adams of note in Colorado history, and one who deserved to have places named after him but apparently didn't, was General Charles Adams (1844–1895). General Adams played a major role in procuring the release of Nathan Meeker's wife and daughter, along with another young woman, after they were taken hostage by a group of renegade Ute Indians during the Meeker Massacre. Although General Adams survived many opportunities to be killed during his travels through the mountains of Colorado in all kinds of weather, he ended up dying in a steam boiler explosion at the Gumry Hotel on Larimer Street in Denver on August 20, 1895.

ALLISON. This name comes from Allison Stocker, a pioneer contractor who constructed many buildings of historical significance in Denver. He was also an active player in what is now La Plata County in far southwest Colorado. This led to his name being given to a town along Colorado Highway 151 on the Southern Ute Indian Reservation established in 1901. The town was originally named Vallejo, but California had already claimed that name; to the great relief of the U.S. Postal Service, the name was changed to Allison.

ARVADA. This name comes from Hiram Arvada Hoskin, who happened to be the brother-in-law of Mary Ann Wadsworth, who happened to be the wife of Benjamin Franklin Wadsworth, who was the guy who founded the town of Arvada around 1870. Wadsworth asked his wife to come up with a name for the town, and she chose her brother-in-law's middle name, Arvada. Benjamin Wadsworth was an energetic promoter of the community and its first postmaster. Wadsworth Boulevard, a major north–south thoroughfare on the west side of Denver running all the way from Broomfield on the north to Littleton on the south, is named after Ben. Although a matter of debate for many years, Arvada is now recognized as the place where gold was first discovered in Colorado, in 1850. Arvada, with a population of some 111,000, has becomes Colorado's seventh-most populous city and takes up parts of both Jefferson and Adams Counties.

AURORA. This is a Latin word meaning "dawn" or "sunrise" and is the name of Colorado's third-largest city, with a population of 325,078 as of the 2010 census. When first established in 1891, the city was named Fletcher after real estate wheeler-dealer Donald Fletcher, who was active in promoting the community. However, Donald Fletcher ran into hard times when the economy tanked with the Panic of 1893, and he departed the city, leaving behind a trail of unhappy creditors. The residents of the city, in 1907, decided that Fletcher was a tacky name and they needed something classier. Aurora was their choice. Aurora is part of the Greater Denver mega-metroplex. It is mostly in Arapahoe and Adams Counties, but a small part of it oozes over into Douglas County.

BELFORD. James Burns Belford was Colorado's first representative to Congress after Colorado became a state in 1876. Before that, he served as a justice of the Colorado Supreme Court. After a failed reelection bid in 1884, Belford practiced law in Denver, where he gained notoriety defending one of Denver's legendary criminals, Soapy Smith. Belford had bright-red hair and gave fiery speeches, which caused him to be known as the "red-headed rooster of the Rockies." This also led to the naming of Mount Belford, the summit of which has a reddish color. Mount Belford, in the Sawatch Range in central Colorado, is the state's nineteenth-highest peak, at 14,197 feet.

BENNETT. This name comes from Hiram Pitt Bennet (1826–1914), who was a prominent Denver lawyer, the first representative to Congress from the Colorado Territory, a Colorado secretary of state while Colorado was still a territory and Denver's postmaster from 1869 to 1874. He also served in Colorado's first state Senate following statehood. For all of that, Bennet, in 1877, had a town east of Denver, in Adams County, named after him. The town of Bennett is to the southeast of Denver International Airport and just a stone's throw north off I-70 as that highway rolls across the Colorado plains on its way to (or from) Kansas. For some reason, the citizens of this town decided to add a second *t* to the name in 1907. To be thorough here, there is another theory running around as to how this town got its name. Per this theory, the town was named after two sisters—maiden name Bennet—who were married to two railroad men, an engineer and a fireman, both of whom were killed in a train accident that

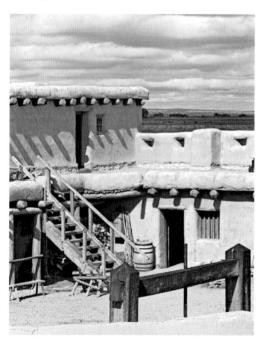

occurred when nearby Kiowa Creek flooded and washed out a bridge. However, since the train accident took place a year after the name Bennet (one *t*) was used for the opening of a post office, the railroad widows theory seems to lack credibility.

BENT. This name ties to William Bent, one of Colorado's first big-time entrepreneurs. William Bent, along with his brother, Charles, and a French fur trader named Césan St. Vrain, built Bent's Fort in 1833. Bent's Fort was a venue for trading with Indian tribes in the area. Bent's Fort is located just north and east of the town of La Junta,

Bent's Fort, Colorado's first shopping mall. *Ealdgyth via Wikimedia Commons.*

106

in southeast Colorado, and is now a museum open to the public. Bent's Fort played a prominent role in James A. Michner's historical novel *Centennial*. Bent County was formed in 1874 and initially covered much of southeast Colorado. However, in 1889, it lost a large chunk of its land to five other nearby counties. One consequence of this is that Bent's Fort is no longer in Bent County. It's in Otero County.

BOETTCHER. This name comes from Charles Boettcher (1852–1948), a German immigrant (at age seventeen) who made a tidy fortune in numerous business enterprises involving, among other things, hardware, mining, cement and sugar beets. His wealth eventually flowed into the Boettcher Foundation, which has helped to fund many noteworthy philanthropic activities in Colorado, including the Boettcher Concert Hall and the Denver Botanic Gardens. There is also a town in north-central Colorado (Larimer County) named Boettcher and, to the west a ways, a lake with this name in Jackson County.

BRECKENRIDGE. This name, in a roundabout way, comes from John Cable Breckinridge (1821–1875). Breckinridge, from Kentucky, was vice president of the United States in 1859 when what is now the town of Breckenridge was founded by a group of prospectors headed by General George E. Spencer. Spencer, who hailed from Alabama, wanted to honor Breckinridge, a fellow southerner, when he named the town. He also thought (correctly, it turned out) that naming the town after the vice president of the United States would improve his chances for obtaining a post office for this remote new community. (The Breckinridge Post Office became the first post office to be established between the Continental Divide and Salt Lake City.) Once the Civil War began, Breckinridge, by then a U.S. senator from Kentucky, declared his allegiance to the Confederacy and became a brigadier general in the Confederate army. The residents of Breckinridge, who were by and large ardent Unionists, weren't happy about this and petitioned Congress to change the name of their town. The name was therefore changed from Breckinridge to Breckenridge, and that seemed to satisfy the locals.

CARR. The Ralph L. Carr Judicial Center in Denver is home of the Colorado Supreme Court and the Colorado Court of Appeals. It is named for Colorado's twenty-ninth governor, who lived from 1887 to 1950. Carr's term as governor was from 1939 to 1943 and overlapped with the beginning of World War II and the attack on Pearl Harbor. After Pearl Harbor, Carr

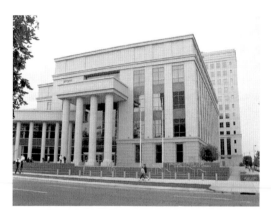

The Colorado Judicial Building in Denver, home of the Colorado Supreme Court and Colorado Court of Appeals and named for Ralph L. Carr, Colorado's twenty-ninth governor who, despite much public criticism, steadfastly opposed Japanese American internment. *Wikimedia Commons.*

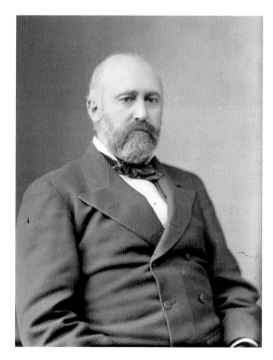

Jerome B. Chaffee, one of Colorado's first two senators after statehood. *Wikimedia Commons.*

steadfastly defended the rights of Colorado's Japanese American residents and (unsuccessfully) opposed their forced removal to detention camps. His position on this issue was unpopular and probably cost him his political career, but he never backed down. Of lesser note, we also have an unincorporated community in northern Weld County named Carr, worthy (just barely) of a post office and a zip code, and occasionally referred to as a ghost town. The name of this community comes from a different Carr: Robert E. Carr, who was president of the Denver Pacific Railroad. The community came into existence when the Denver Pacific established rail service between Denver and Cheyenne, Wyoming, in the early 1870s.

CHAFFEE. This name comes from Jerome B. Chaffee (1825–1886). Chaffee was a successful wheeler-dealer who helped to found the city of Denver, the First National Bank of Denver and the Colorado Territory. From 1871 to 1875, Chaffee served as the Colorado Territory's delegate to Congress. Then, in 1876, when Colorado became a state, he was elected as one of the state's first two U.S. senators. He served one term, and that, apparently, was enough, since he didn't seek reelection. On the trivia front, he had a daughter who married Ulysses S. Grant Jr., a son of the United States president. Chaffee died at his daughter and son-in-law's home in Westchester County, New York, in 1886 at the age of sixty. A county in central Colorado, in one of the most beautiful parts of the state, was named after him in 1879.

CHATFIELD. This name comes from Lieutenant Isaac W. Chatfield (1836–1921), who came to Colorado in the 1860s after serving as a Union army officer in the Civil War. Chatfield eventually bought seven hundred acres of land where the South Platte River and Plum Creek meet and thereby became a successful real estate investor. He moved away in 1879, but his name lives on in the form of Chatfield Dam, Chatfield Reservoir and Chatfield State Park, all on the south side of Littleton. The massive dam was started in 1967, after a devastating flood rolled through the area in 1965 (a follow-up to devastating floods in 1933, 1935 and 1942). It took eight years to complete the project. The reservoir is part of the Denver water system and also a popular recreation site. It has also become a notable hangout for birds of a different feather. More than two hundred bird species have been identified at the reservoir and the park. Some of these stay all year. Others just stop by to visit friends during an annual migration.

CHEESMAN. This name comes from Walter Scott Cheesman (1838–1907). Cheesman was born in New York, spent some time in Chicago and then, in 1861, traveled from there to Denver in an ox cart. He initially joined his brother in a drugstore business but soon moved on to railroads and real estate, becoming a wealthy man and a mover and shaker in the Denver community. The current Colorado Governor's Mansion is a structure originally started by Cheesman shortly before his death. Cheesman was one of the founders of the Denver Chamber of Commerce and was instrumental in the development of important parts of the water storage and delivery systems that serve Denver to this day, including Cheesman Dam and Reservoir along the South Platte River west of the town of Deckers. The South Platte River, as it exits the reservoir and flows through Cheesman Canyon, is a world-famous trout fishery, inhabited by some of the world's most finicky fish. Cheesman Park in Denver is also named after Walter Scott Cheesman.

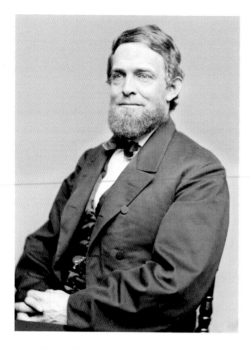

Schuyler Colfax, seventeenth vice president of the United States. Colfax Avenue in Denver, for better or for worse, perpetuates his name. *Wikimedia Commons.*

COLFAX. This name comes from Schuyler Colfax (1823–1885). Colfax, from Indiana, served as the seventeenth vice president of the United States during the presidential term of Ulysses S. Grant (1869–73). A town named Colfax existed in the Denver area from 1891 to 1895. However, it was soon gobbled up by fast-growing Denver. We still have (for better or for worse) Colfax Avenue in Denver, helping to generate traffic congestion but at least running in a straight east–west direction, unlike many of Denver's main roadways. Also of note, German immigrants coming to the Wet Mountain Valley in 1870 with the intention of establishing a cooperative community named their town Colfax. But this town, and the attempt at a cooperative community, didn't last long. The town's communal store and everything in it was, early on, destroyed by a gunpowder explosion. The town's population then quietly disbursed throughout the Wet Mountain Valley, and the town was no more.

CRAIG. This name comes from Reverend William Bayard Craig. Craig, along with others, formed the Craig Land and Mercantile Company in the late 1880s. That company, in turn, laid out the site for what is now the town of Craig and gave the town its name. Craig is in far northwest Colorado, is surrounded by elk that outnumber the people and is the county seat of Moffat County. Reverend Craig was related by marriage to the wife of Colorado's last territorial governor and first state governor, John Routt. Craig came to Denver in 1882 and, before he went into the rural land development business, served as pastor at a few Denver churches. Later on, Reverend Craig left the wilds of western Colorado and returned to Des Moines, Iowa, to serve as chancellor of Drake University.

CRAWFORD. This name comes from George A. Crawford (1827–1891). Crawford was born in Pennsylvania but ended up in Kansas, where he was elected governor in 1861. However, the election was declared illegal, so he never took office. Having apparently then had enough of Kansas, Crawford came to western Colorado, where, among other things, he founded the city of Grand Junction in 1882. There is a small town (population 431 per the 2010 census) in Delta County and a reservoir near that town named after Crawford.

DENVER. The name Denver as used throughout Colorado comes from James W. Denver. He was governor of the Kansas Territory at the time the fast-growing city of Denver received its current name in 1858. General William Larimer, a land speculator from eastern Kansas, chose this name for his new city in the hope of winning favors from Governor Denver. Today, the municipality of Denver functions under a consolidated city-county form of government, which helps to avoid the snarling between city councils and county commissioners that regularly takes place in other parts of the state. Denver has a rich and colorful history, including a period, 1880–95, when it was a hotbed of corruption, with crime bosses such as Soapy Smith getting together with elected government officials to nurture a vibrant crime- and graft-based economy. In case you're wondering, folksinger John Denver ("Rocky Mountain High," "Take Me Home, Country Roads," "Annie's Song," "Sunshine on My Shoulders," "Montana Skies" and so on) was actually named

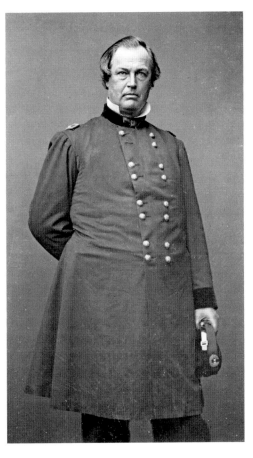

James W. Denver, the governor of the Territory of Kansas in 1858 when the city of Denver was first named. *Wikimedia Commons.*

Henry John Deutschendorf Jr. He died in 1997 when an experimental plane he was flying crashed into Monterey Bay. There is a touching John Denver memorial next to the Roaring Fork River as it runs along the east side of downtown Aspen that is worth a visit.

Douglas. Use of this name in Colorado comes from two people. First, we have Stephen Arnold Douglas (1813–1861), a U.S. senator from Illinois from 1849 to 1861 who is most famous for losing the 1860 presidential election to Abraham Lincoln. (It should be noted, however, that Douglas had earlier defeated Lincoln in a senatorial election.) Douglas County is named after Senator Douglas. Unfortunately, Douglas didn't live long enough to enjoy this honor. He died in 1861, five months before the county was created as one of the original seventeen counties that made up the Colorado Territory. When first established, the county extended all the way to the Kansas border. But in 1874, a large chunk of its east side was lopped off to create Elbert County. As for the second Douglas, we have a Ute Indian chief who was called Douglas by white settlers (but probably not by his mother). This Douglas is famous because in 1879 warriors under his command killed Indian agent Nathan Meeker and several of his employees in what became known as the Meeker Massacre. In punishment for that event, Chief Douglas spent nearly a year in prison at Fort Leavenworth, Kansas. He died in 1885 in a fight with another tribal member. Douglas Pass in remote northwestern Colorado is named after Chief Douglas and not Senator Douglas. This pass is along scenic Colorado Highway 139 and has an elevation of 8,268 feet.

Elizabeth. This name comes from the sister-in-law of Colorado territorial governor John Evans. Evans was a wealthy guy who, among other things, owned the Denver and New Orleans Railroad, which gave him the right to name towns along its tracks. One night, Evans was having dinner with his wife, Margaret, and Margaret's sister, Elizabeth, at the Evans's opulent residence in Denver. At some point during the evening, the subject of naming towns along the rail line came up, and Evans told Elizabeth he would name a town after her, which he did. Elizabeth is a quiet little community in Elbert County that is still rural in nature despite its proximity to the sprawl of Denver. The area is a popular place for people to live who have chosen to greatly complicate their life and greatly diminish their net worth by owning horses.

Elbert. The name Elbert comes from Samuel Hitt Elbert (1833–1899). Elbert was the governor of the Colorado Territory in 1873 and 1874, and then, after Colorado became a state in 1876, he served as chief justice of the Colorado Supreme Court from 1879 to 1883. Elbert was instrumental in organizing the Republican Party in Colorado (which may explain his appointment to high judicial office). Elbert County, carved out of the eastern part of neighboring Douglas County, was formed in 1874, while Colorado was still a territory. Although largely rural, Elbert County is close enough to Denver to be a part of the Denver-Aurora Metropolitan Statistical Area. Colorado's highest mountain, Mount Elbert (14,440 feet, or if you're from, say, Canada, 4,401 meters), was named after Elbert in apparent appreciation for his having negotiated a deal with the Ute Indians that opened up some 3 million acres of reservation land to mining and railroading. (It is likely this was a deal the Utes later came to regret.)

ESTES. This name comes from Joel Estes, a Missouri gold seeker turned rancher who founded the town of Estes Park in 1859, notwithstanding the regular use of this area by hostile Indian tribes over hundreds of years. Estes Park was one of Colorado's first tourist destinations, and as the eastern gateway to Rocky Mountain National Park, tourism continues to be the economic lifeblood of the community. Estes Park is also the site of the stately, and world-famous, Stanley Hotel, which promotes itself as being haunted and was the inspiration for the Overlook Hotel in Stephen King's novel *The Shining*. Nearby Lake Estes is a reservoir formed as part of the forever controversial Colorado–Big Thompson trans-mountain water diversion project, which brings water from the west side of the Continental Divide to the east side through an elaborate system of dams, tunnels and pumps.

EVANS. This name comes from John Evans (1814–1897). He was the second governor of the Colorado Territory. John Evans is best known for founding Evanston, Illinois; Northwestern University; and the University of Denver. Mount Evans, a part of the collection of mountains known as the Front Range, tops out at 14,264 feet, placing it fourteenth on Colorado's highest mountains list. The mountain was originally named Mount Rosalie in 1863 by western landscape painter Albert Bierstadt in honor of his wife. But Rosalie lost out to Evans, at least informally, in 1870. The Colorado legislature then made the name change official in 1895, on Evans's eighty-first birthday. There is also a town named Evans in north-central Colorado (Weld County).

FLAGLER. This name comes from Henry M. Flagler, a railroad and oil entrepreneur who had the good sense to become a longtime associate of

John D. Rockefeller in connection with the Standard Oil Company. The small community of Flagler, in Kit Carson County on the state's far east side, was originally known as Bowser, after the favorite dog of a local merchant. It was then named Malowe, after a railroad lawyer named M.A. Lowe, before the Flagler name was finally adopted.

FLORENCE. This name, given to a town in Fremont County, Colorado, to the south and east of Cañon City, comes from the daughter of James A. McCandless. McCandless, in the 1860s, operated an oil refinery in the area, processing oil from an oil field he owned. This was America's second-oldest oil field. In 1872, McCandless donated land that became the official town site for Florence, in appreciation for which he received naming rights for the town. Prior to that time, the town had been called Frazerville, for a local coal mine developer known as Uncle Joe Frazer.

FOWLER. This name comes from Orson Squire Fowler (1809–1887), who, among other things, was a well-known proponent of the pseudoscience of phrenology. Phrenologists were a big deal in the mid-1800s. They believed the human brain had a distinct set of sectors—like apps on a cellphone—each of which had a specific function. There were twenty-seven of these, and phrenologists claimed they could map them all with a hands-on exploration of the skull. Orson Fowler was also ahead of his time as a proponent of organic farming (and healthy country living), and that's apparently what brought him from the East Coast to southeast Colorado. Shortly before his death in 1887, he bought some land along the Arkansas River in what is now Otero County and started a town. The town was originally named Oxford because a large ox managed to get itself killed trying to cross the tracks of the Atchison, Topeka and Santa Fe Railroad. However, there was already a town named Oxford along this same rail line, leading to a change in the name of the town to Fowler. Orson Fowler didn't get to enjoy this tribute. He was already dead by the time the name change occurred.

FRUITA. This name (pronounced froo-tah) comes from, well, fruit. In the early 1880s, a man named William Pabor recognized the fruit growing potential of a valley in western Colorado along the Colorado River, so he started a town there, heavily promoted the town to easterners eager to relocate west, sold land and organized a community having similarities to the largely unsuccessful Union Colony, an experiment in communal living that eventually morphed into Greeley, Colorado. Pabor had been involved in the development of Union Colony, and one of the attributes of that community he brought with him to Fruita was a ban on the sale or manufacture of alcohol. The residents of Fruita finally threw this restriction out in a vote held in the 1970s. Fruita, which sits along Interstate 70 between Grand Junction and the Utah border, was originally named Fruitdale. It is near the Colorado National Monument, in an area now famous for important paleontological discoveries. The town even has a dinosaur named after it—the *Fruitadens*. This is the world's smallest known plant-eating dinosaur, topping out at thirty inches in length and 1.7 pounds, the dinosaur equivalent of a lap dog.

GARFIELD. We can thank James A. Garfield (1831–1881), twentieth president of the United States, for widespread use of the Garfield name in Colorado. Garfield was elected president in 1881 and lasted all of two hundred days in office before he was assassinated by a wacko lawyer and religious fanatic named Charles J. Guiteau, who was hanged for his crime. Despite the short duration of his presidency, Garfield had several accomplishments to his credit, including purging the United States Post Office of rampant corruption. Garfield County, in west-central Colorado, was created in 1883 by means of a carve-out from Summit County and was named for the deceased president.

GILPIN. This names comes from Colonel William Gilpin, who was a military officer, explorer, politician and land speculator—another interesting combination of skills. He served as Colorado's first territorial governor, appointed to this position by President Lincoln in 1861. Gilpin lasted only a year at this job, thanks in part to his having issued $375,000 of drafts on the United States Treasury without authority to do so. When the United States Treasury refused to honor these drafts, Gilpin's career in politics quickly ended. Thereafter, Gilpin managed to accumulate substantial wealth dealing in real estate in New Mexico. His real estate activities there have been described as ethically questionable and possibly illegal. Before concerns about his behavior surfaced, Gilpin's name was given to a Colorado county. Gilpin County, situated to the north and west a bit from the Denver metropolitan area, was created in 1861 as one of the original seventeen counties making up the Colorado Territory. It is Colorado's second-smallest county. The county seat for Gilpin County is Central City, founded in 1859 as a mining town during the Pikes Peak gold rush and originally named Mountain City. Central City today is best known for its opera house, as well as for limited-stakes gambling in competition with next-door neighbor Black Hawk.

GRANBY. This name comes from Granby Hillyer, a Colorado lawyer who, during his legal career, served as a Colorado District Court judge, a U.S. attorney for Colorado and a state legislator. For unknown reasons, the Frontier Land and Investment Company, developer of the town in Grand County now known as Granby, engaged Hillyer in 1904 to lay out the streets for this new town. Hillyer, however, had no training or aptitude for this sort of work, something current residents of the town readily acknowledge. In any event, the town was named after Hillyer. We now also have Lake Granby, named after the town. Lake Granby is a reservoir formed by the construction of Granby Dam in 1950 as part of the Colorado–Big Thompson trans-mountain water diversion project.

GREELEY. This name comes from Horace Greeley (1811–1872), best known as the outspoken editor of the once influential *New York Tribune*. The city of Greeley came about because Horace Greeley made a trip to Colorado in 1859 and was impressed by what he saw—an area where the South Platte River comes out of the mountains and onto the plains having, Greeley thought, enormous agricultural potential. A few years later, the agricultural editor of the *Tribune*, Nathan C. Meeker (of Meeker Massacre fame), came to the site and, with Horace Greeley's backing, started a utopian communal living experiment known as Union Colony. Overall, Union Colony proved to be a bad idea, and it eventually morphed into the city of Greeley, a typical Colorado cow town with no greater moral pretentions than any other frontier settlement (although it did continue to

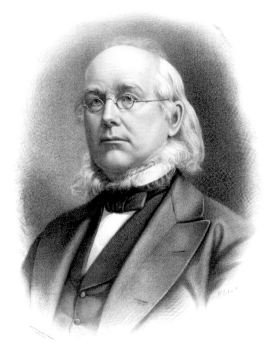

Horace Greeley, who on a trip to Colorado in 1859 decided that, with some help from irrigation, there was agricultural potential on the east side of the mountains, causing him to bankroll the Union Colony shared resources experiment. *Wikimedia Commons.*

ban alcohol for a while after Prohibition ended). Horace Greeley ran for president in 1872 as the candidate of the new Liberal Republican Party and with support from the Democratic Party. The election went to Ulysses S. Grant in a landslide, and Greeley died three weeks later.

GUANELLA. This name comes from Byron Guanella (1913–1984). Guanella was a longtime county commissioner in Clear Creek County and served as that county's road supervisor. A mountain pass, connecting Interstate 70 on the north and U.S. Highway 285 on the south, was named in his honor in 1953. Guanella had planned the route over the pass. Guanella Pass rises to 11,669 feet, putting it eighth on the list of Colorado mountain passes with an improved road (or seventh if you don't count the high point on Trail Ridge Road as a pass). The pass was closed for a few years following a 2007 landslide, but it is now open again (other than in the winter) and can be driven in a standard passenger vehicle by people who are tolerant of washboard surfaces and willing to shorten the life of their shock absorbers. A popular trailhead to Mount Bierstadt, one of Colorado's fourteeners, is located at the top of Guanella Pass.

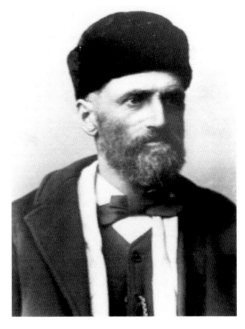

HARTSEL. This name comes from Samuel Hartsel (1834–1918), who came to South Park from Pennsylvania around 1860. Hartsel, like everyone at the time, was a wannabe miner in search of gold. But he soon realized a more reliable source of income came from selling things like, say, food to miners. Starting with a 160-acre homestead property, Hartsel built up a ranch spanning some 10,000 acres, and along the way, he developed a sawmill, trading post, blacksmith shop and hotel. The big attraction for the hotel was a hot spring in the area, which he commercialized with a bathhouse.

Samuel Hartsel, who expanded a 160-acre homestead into a 10,000-acre ranch and operated multiple successful businesses in an unlikely place: South Park, Colorado. *Park County Local History Archives.*

117

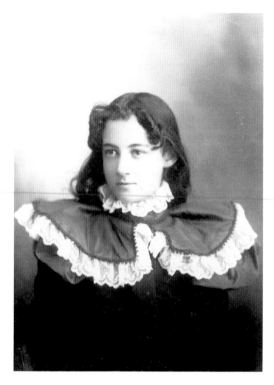

Left: Samuel Hartsel's daughter, Henrietta, apparently given time off from her normal ranching chores for this photo shoot. *Park County Local History Archives*.

Below: Government efficiency at work in Hartsel, Colorado. *Photo by author*.

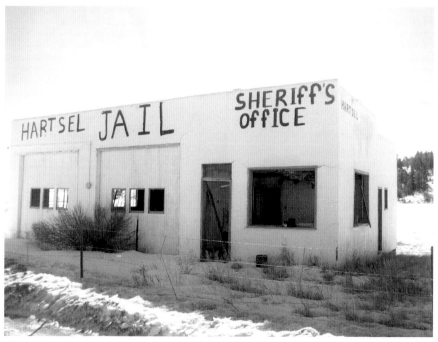

Although in disrepair (and unlikely to meet with the approval of any public health agencies in the area), the remnants of the bathhouse still exist just to the south of the town of Hartsel. The town is located at the intersection of U.S. Highway 24 and Colorado Highway 9 and is a small outpost of civilization at the west end of the main expanse of South Park. You can buy gasoline here at a price reflecting the fact that this is not a good place to run out. The only other gas station around is twenty miles to the north, in Fairplay.

HINSDALE. This name comes from George A. Hinsdale (1826–1874). Hinsdale was born in Vermont and eventually headed west. After practicing law in Nebraska for a while and serving in that state's legislature, he packed up his wife and children, put them in an ox cart and headed to Colorado in 1860 to chase gold in the Leadville area. Seemingly unsuccessful in that enterprise, he spent time in Cañon City and San Luis and eventually ended up in Pueblo, where he developed a significant presence in the community, helping to found the first church in the area and serving as county attorney. In 1865, he held office as lieutenant governor for the Colorado Territory. Hindsdale died in 1874, two years before Colorado became a state. Hinsdale County was named in his honor that same year. This county was carved out of previously established Lake, Conejos and Costilla Counties. It is the least densely populated county in Colorado. The Continental Divide crosses Hinsdale County in two places. The county has numerous wilderness areas and fourteen-thousand-foot peaks. (I can also report that beautiful, and sometimes large, brook trout live in the high mountain lakes of Hinsdale County. However, these fish have greater intelligence than they are usually given credit for and can be very particular about what they eat.)

JULESBURG. This name comes from Jules Beni. In the early 1860s, Beni ran a trading post in far northeast Colorado along the Pony Express route between Missouri and California. Beni was also an alleged horse thief who, after several shootouts, was finally ambushed and gruesomely killed by Jack Slade, a superintendent with the Pikes Peak Express Company whose horses Slade thought Beni had been stealing. The town of Julesburg is the county seat of Sedgwick County and a stone's throw away from the Colorado/Nebraska line. Mark Twain's travelogue, *Roughing It*, devotes several pages to the exploits of Jack Slade, who, at least according to Twain, seems to have been the nineteenth-century equivalent of a bloodthirsty terrorist.

KEN CARYL. This name, given to a large planned development to the west of Littleton and Interstate 470, comes from the Ken Caryl ranch, previously owned by newspaper magnate John C. Shaffer (*Rocky Mountain News*). Shaffer named the ranch after his two sons, Kent and Carrol. (I haven't found an explanation for how Carrol became Caryl.) Shaffer lost the ranch to creditors during the Great Depression.

KREMMLING. This name came from Rudolph "Kare" Kremmling, who opened a general store along the upper Colorado River in the early 1880s, when the Colorado silver rush was rolling along at full speed. In the beginning, this store was all there was in the way of a settlement. After the settlement grew a bit, Mr. Kremmling became its first postmaster, and the town eventually took his name. Initially, however, the town was called Kinsey City, after brothers Aaron and John Kinsey, who provided a portion of their ranch land for the town site.

LAMAR. This name comes from Lucius Quintus Cincinnatus Lamar (1825–1893), who was secretary of the interior in the cabinet of President Grover Cleveland during his first term in office. In 1886, Lamar's name was given to a town along the Arkansas River east of Pueblo (and east of La Junta) by a Garden City, Kansas land speculator named I.R. Holmes. Holmes was maneuvering to have a federal land office established at this location, and naming the town Lamar was a blatant—and apparently successful—attempt on his part to influence the decision. Once the land office was in place, Holmes used it as a base from which to sell lots to people back in Kansas. Lucius Q.C. Lamar, who may never have seen the town bearing his name, went on to be a justice of the United States Supreme Court, where he served from 1888 until his death in 1893.

LARIMER. The name Larimer appears many places in Colorado thanks to William Larimer Jr. (1809–1875). Larimer was, among other things, a land speculator. He came to what would become the Colorado Territory from Kansas in the late 1850s and is considered one of the founders of Denver. He was also instrumental in the formation of the Colorado Territory in 1861. Larimer had hopes of becoming the first governor of the Colorado Territory, but President Abraham Lincoln gave that job to William Gilpin instead. Larimer County, in north-central Colorado, was one of the original seventeen Colorado counties formed in 1861. The county soon thereafter found itself in a legal dispute over the location of its western boundary.

The Colorado Supreme Court resolved the dispute in 1886, and Larimer County prevailed in its position. In 1909, however, the county lost the land it had litigated to keep to Jackson County, with politics trumping law. The city of Fort Collins is the largest municipality in Larimer County and the county seat.

LITTLETON. This name came from Richard Sullivan Little (1829–1899), a civil engineer from New Hampshire who came to Colorado during the Colorado gold rush days (which began in earnest in 1859) and found himself busy doing land surveying and working on irrigation systems. He then settled in the area that is now the city of Littleton and, with others, built and operated an important economic driver for the community, the Rough and Ready Flour Mill. For the rest of his life, Little was active in the development of the city that now bears his name. Following his death in December 1899, his funeral procession was the largest such event ever to have occurred in this part of Colorado. Littleton lies to the west of Denver and spreads out among Arapahoe, Douglas and Jefferson Counties, leading to a predictable amount of governmental chaos.

LOGAN. This name shows up in Colorado (and elsewhere) in recognition of the accomplishments of John Alexander Logan (1826–1886), a noted general in the Union army during the Civil War. After the war, Logan was a representative, and then a senator, from Illinois. He was an unsuccessful candidate for vice president in 1884 on the ticket of Republican James G. Blaine. (I'm sure you remember him.) Logan is one of the three people—along with Abraham Lincoln and Ulysses S. Grant—mentioned in the official Illinois state song. He was also a moving force in the creation of Memorial Day as a national holiday. Although his ties to Colorado are tenuous (or nonexistent), a county in northeastern Colorado was named after him in 1887, a year after his death. Logan County was formerly a part of Weld County.

LOVELAND. This name honors the accomplishments of William A.H. Loveland (1826–1894). This included service as the president of the Colorado Central Railroad, a stint as mayor of the city of Golden, helping to found the Colorado School of Mines, development of the city of Lakewood and ownership (as the second owner) of the *Rocky Mountain News*. The city of Loveland, in north-central Colorado, was founded in 1877 and ranks somewhere around fourteenth in the state in population. Loveland has given itself a nickname—the "Sweetheart City"—and likes to be the place from which valentines are mailed, bearing a Loveland postmark. Once upon a time, Loveland was a large producer of cherries. By 1960, however, various malevolent acts of Mother Nature had shut down this industry. Loveland Pass, rising to 11,990 feet, holds fifth place on the list of Colorado mountain passes crossed by a paved or gravel road—in this case U.S. Highway 6, paved in both directions. (Loveland Pass is in fourth position if you don't count the high point along Trail Ridge Road in Rocky Mountain National Park as a pass.) Until the Eisenhower Tunnel was finally completed in 1979, vehicles traveling between Denver and the Western Slope had to use Loveland Pass, resulting in lots of winter driving excitement. This is still the case if you're driving a truck loaded with explosives and are therefore not allowed to use the Eisenhower Tunnel.

LUPTON. This name comes from Lieutenant Lancaster P. Lupton (1807–1885), a West Point graduate who resigned his army commission to start a trading post along the South Platte River in 1840 near where the town of Fort Lupton, in what is now Weld County, is located. Lieutenant Lupton apparently got along well with the Indians in the area since he married the daughter of one of their chiefs—a woman named Tomas. A horrific blizzard in 1844 chased Lupton and Tomas out of the area and shut down the trading post. The Luptons thereupon moved to a location near Pueblo, where they stayed for a few years. Then they headed to California around 1849 when the California gold rush hit full stride. Lupton and Tomas, no doubt remembering the blizzard of 1844, remained in California until Lupton's death in 1885.

LYONS. This name comes from Edward S. Lyon, who started a town in 1880 at the confluence of North Saint Vrain Creek and South Saint Vrain Creek, some twenty miles east of what would become Rocky Mountain National Park. Lyon was attracted to the area by the easily quarried red sandstone he found there. This sandstone is still being mined and is widely used as a decorative product. No one seems to know when, or why, the *s* was added to the name of the town. Lyons was ground zero for a devastating flash flood that occurred on September 13, 2013.

MARTIN. John A. Martin (1868–1939) was an attorney, onetime publisher of the *La Junta Times* and a politician who served as a U.S. representative from Colorado on two occasions, 1909–13 and 1933–39. His name lives on with a state park and reservoir in southeast (Bent County) Colorado.

MᴄPʜᴇᴇ. This name comes from William McPhee, a Denver businessman who, in the 1920s, was instrumental in starting a lumber company—the New Mexico Lumber Company—in southwest Colorado. This led to the formation of a small town near the company's sawmill, which was given the name McPhee. The lumber company operated until the 1940s and then shut down. However, the McPhee name lives on with McPhee Reservoir, Colorado's fourth-largest reservoir (if you don't include Navajo Reservoir, which is partly in Colorado and partly in New Mexico) and the adjacent McPhee Recreation Area. The reservoir was formed by a dam across the Dolores River, completed in 1985. The original town site for McPhee, Colorado, is now at the bottom of the reservoir, so don't plan a visit.

Mᴇᴇᴋᴇʀ. This name comes from Nathan Meeker who (to his ultimate regret) sought and was given the position of Indian agent for several bands of Ute Indians living in northwest and west-central Colorado, principally along the White River. Meeker's attempts at turning the Utes into farmers didn't go well, and in 1879, he was savagely murdered by a small renegade group of them in what became known as the Meeker Massacre. Prior to his Indian agent assignment, Meeker was deeply involved, as an associate of Horace Greeley, in the Union Colony, an experiment in communal living that also didn't go particularly well and left Meeker substantially in debt. The Union Colony

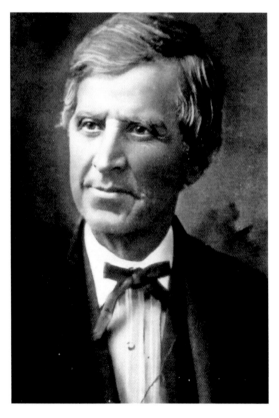

Nathan Meeker, who, using Horace Greeley's money, made history by getting the Union Colony up and running and who made even more history by getting himself killed by renegade Ute Indians during the Meeker Massacre. *Brooks, S., Greeley History for Kids, http://greeleyhistory.org.*

eventually became the city of Greeley. The town of Meeker, county seat of Rio Blanco County, is the gateway to the Flat Tops Wilderness and a favorite destination for hunters, fishermen, snowmobilers and other outdoor adventurers. Teddy Roosevelt once visited Meeker on a mountain lion–hunting trip and stayed at the still-in-business Meeker Hotel.

MILNER. There are two Milners whose names have been preserved by Colorado places. F.E. Milner was a pioneering banker and merchant in north-central Colorado. The unincorporated town of Milner, not far from the Steamboat Springs ski area in Routt County, is named after him. Then there's T.J. Milner, a surveyor and engineer who helped survey what is now Trail Ridge Road (U.S. Highway 34), traversing Rocky Mountain National Park. Milner Pass, along Trail Ridge Road, is named after him. Milner Pass rises to 10,759 feet, putting it twenty-sixth on the list of Colorado mountain passes with improved (asphalt or gravel) roads. The highest point on Trail Ridge Road has an elevation of 12,183 feet, making it, arguably, the highest paved road pass in Colorado. But because that area is relatively flat, it doesn't seem to qualify as a pass and has never been given a pass name. This has allowed Independence Pass, at 12,095 feet, to lay claim to being the highest paved road pass in Colorado. Cottonwood Pass, at 12,126 feet, is arguably in the hunt for this title. However, only the east side of Cottonwood Pass is served by a paved road. From the summit on westward, the road is gravel.

MOFFAT. This name comes from David Halliday Moffat (1839–1911), a Denver banker, financier, industrialist and dreamer who accumulated substantial wealth and then spent most of it trying, unsuccessfully, to build a railroad line that would connect Denver to Salt Lake City. Although Pueblo and Cheyenne had rail lines heading directly west to Salt Lake City, Denver did not. Moffat wanted to fix that. He died in New York City in 1911 while trying to raise additional funds for his railroad venture. Finally, in 1928, a 6.2-mile tunnel cutting through the Continental Divide was completed, allowing for construction of the rail route Moffat had hoped to create. In apparent appreciation for his valiant, but failed, effort, this tunnel was named after him. In addition to permitting rail transportation west out of Denver, Moffat Tunnel is home to a major water line delivering water from the mountains west of the Continental Divide to the Denver area. David Moffat also had a county named after him in 1911, the year he died. Moffat County is in the far northwest corner of Colorado. It was created out of land taken from Routt County. And, the small town of Moffat can be found in sparsely populated Saguache County, in south-central Colorado. The town was established in 1890 along the tracks of the narrow-gauge Denver and Rio Grande Railway. At that time, it was a major shipping point for cattle raised in the area.

MORRISON. This name came from George Morrison (1822–1895), an early settler in the foothills west of Denver who, in 1874, platted the site for the town that now bears his name. Morrison was a stonemason, and his company, Morrison Stone, Lime and Town Company, brought fame to the area as a source of much sought-after building materials. These days, the town is best known for its nearby neighbor, Red Rocks Amphitheatre, a popular (in the summer) entertainment venue.

NORTHGLENN. This name was invented by the developers of a large shopping mall that was located, well, north of Denver. In addition to the Northglenn Mall, the company (Perl-Mack) also created a town in the area and gave it the same name. Showing similar imagination, the company later developed a shopping mall south of Denver and named it Southglenn. Northglenn is now a part of the I-25 corridor sprawl between Denver and Loveland. It has grown in size to rank twenty-first among Colorado cities, based on population.

ORDWAY. This name comes from George N. Ordway, a Denver businessman who bought land fifty miles east of Pueblo, in Crowley County, and started a town there in the 1890s. One story has it that to choose a name for the town, the names of three town promoters were placed in a hat; Ordway won the drawing.

OTERO. This name shows up often in Colorado thanks to Miguel Antonio Otero (1829–1882). During his short life of fifty-one years, Otero held many prominent government positions in the New Mexico Territory, including service as a representative in Congress. His political career stalled out in the 1860s due in part to a perceived pro-Confederate loyalty. He then, however, went on to become a successful entrepreneur, with profitable interests in banking, farming and railroads. His son, also named Miguel Antonio Otero (nickname "Gillie"), became governor of the New Mexico Territory after his father's death. (New Mexico didn't become a state until 1912.) Otero County, in southeast Colorado, came into being in 1889 in a split-up of Bent County. Miguel Otero, the elder, helped to found the town of La Junta, chartered in 1881, the year before his death. La Junta is now a city and the county seat of Otero County. Otero Savings and Loan was a significant Colorado banking enterprise until the collapse of the savings and loan industry in the late 1980s and early 1990s. It owned an elegant collection of western art.

Palmer. This name comes from General William Jackson Palmer (1836–1909), an extraordinary man who was hugely important in the development of Colorado. Palmer was a civil engineer, soldier, industrialist and generous philanthropist who first came to the Colorado Territory as a surveyor for the

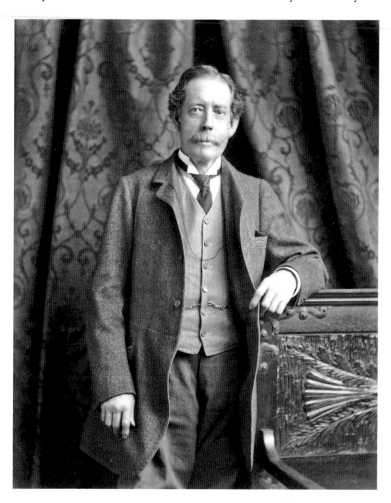

General William Palmer, the founder of Colorado Springs and the driving force behind the Denver and Rio Grande Railway. *Colorado Springs Pioneers Museum.*

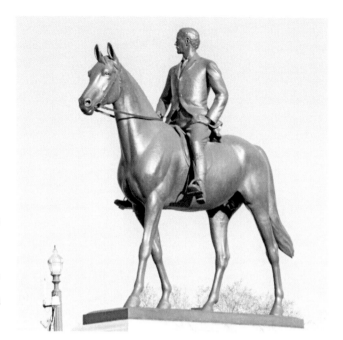

This elegant statue of General Palmer on his horse sits in the middle of a busy intersection in Colorado Springs, where it regularly causes traffic accidents. Palmer spent the last three years of his life in a wheelchair thanks to a horse. *Photo by author.*

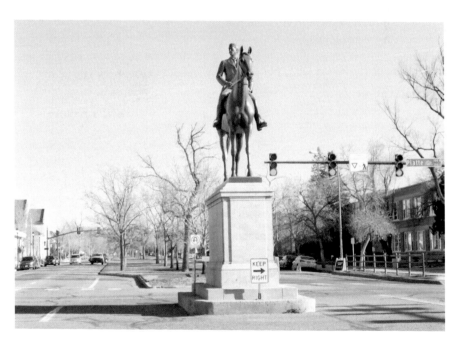

Here's the Palmer-on-horse statue, showing the intersection where it sits. Photo taken early on a Sunday morning when it was reasonably safe to be there. *Photo by author.*

Kansas Pacific Railway. He was a co-founder (along with an Englishman named Dr. William Bell) of the Denver and Rio Grande Railway; founded the cities of Colorado Springs, Manitou Springs and Fountain; and was involved in the formation of Colorado Fuel and Iron, a Pueblo-based steel manufacturing company (eventually controlled by the Rockefeller family) that resulted from the merger of Palmer's Colorado Coal and Iron Company with the Colorado Coal Company. Palmer built a magnificent home, Glen Eyre, just to the north of the Garden of the Gods, that now serves as headquarters for the Navigators, a nonprofit Christian organization with worldwide activities. Palmer's wife, whose real name was Mary but who was known by everyone as Queen, permanently left Colorado Springs in 1885 because of a heart condition (and perhaps in pursuit of better shopping opportunities) and relocated to London. General Palmer himself remained in Colorado Springs. He broke his spine in an equestrian accident in 1906 and spent the last three years of his life in a wheelchair. A large and handsome statue of Palmer, seated on his horse, sits in the middle of the intersection of Nevada Avenue and Platte Avenue in Colorado Springs. It has been the cause of hundreds—perhaps thousands—of traffic accidents since its installation.

PENROSE. This name comes from Spencer Penrose (1865–1939). Penrose was born into a prominent Philadelphia family and attended Harvard, where he earned the distinction of graduating last in the class of 1886. Penrose was an astute (and lucky) entrepreneur who accumulated a huge fortune through timely investments in real estate, mining and other ventures. Most notably, his purchase of land in Utah containing vast quantities of low-grade copper ore, coupled with the development of technology that allowed the copper to be profitably extracted, produced much of his wealth. In addition to enjoying his wealth through personal indulgences (like, say, polo) and constructing the luxurious Broadmoor Hotel as a place to hang out and drink with his friends, Penrose, with help from his wife, Julie, contributed much to the community of Colorado Springs as a philanthropist. The Cheyenne Mountain Zoo and the Colorado Springs Fine Arts Center, for example, were made possible by the Penroses' generosity. And Penrose Hospital has long been, and continues to be, a healthcare fixture in Colorado Springs. Spencer Penrose was also a key player in the construction of a road to the summit of Pikes Peak— the Pikes Peak Highway—and the creation of the town of Penrose, south of Colorado Springs and east of Cañon City, along the U.S. Highway 50 corridor, known for its apple orchards. Penrose planned to call this town Fremont, but the residents named it after him instead.

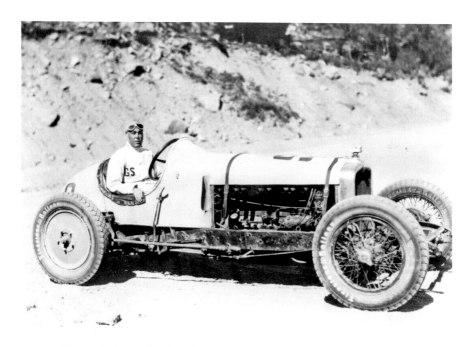

Spencer Penrose helped to build the Pikes Peak Highway. The Pikes Peak Hill Climb, an internationally famous automobile and motorcycle race up the highway to the top of Pikes Peak, celebrated its 100th anniversary in 2016. Here's a hill climb race car from earlier times. Today's cars are modestly safer and a great deal faster. *Colorado Springs Pioneers Museum.*

PITKIN. This name comes from Frederick Walker Pitkin (1837–1886). He was the second governor of the state of Colorado. Pitkin, a lawyer who first set up shop in Wisconsin, moved to southwest Colorado in 1874 and managed to make some timely bets in the mining industry. With help from his contacts in that industry, he was elected governor in 1878 on the Republican ticket and ended up serving two terms. During his time as governor, Pitkin had to deal with railroad wars, Indian uprisings and strikes by mineworkers in the Leadville area. He ran for the United States Senate in 1882, unsuccessfully, and thereafter retreated to the practice of law in Pueblo, Colorado. Pitkin County was formed in 1881. This county, in west-central Colorado, is most famous for the town of Aspen, its county seat. Because the rich and famous discovered Aspen as a cool place to hang out several decades ago, Pitkin County has one of the highest per capita incomes of any county in the country.

RHODA. This name comes from Rhoda Krasner. Rhoda's father, Adam Krasner, rescued the Lakeside Amusement Park from bankruptcy during the Great Depression, and since the lake (which is a natural lake) is right next to the amusement park, Adam named it after his daughter. Prior to that, Rhoda Lake was known as West Berkeley Lake.

ROBERTS. This name comes from Harold D. Roberts, a prominent Denver lawyer who was a member of the Denver Board of Water Commissioners (known widely as just "Denver Water"). Roberts was instrumental in pushing through to completion a plan to divert water from the west side of the Continental Divide to the Denver metropolitan area. This included the construction of Dillon Dam and Dillon Reservoir, as well as a twenty-three-mile-long/ten-foot-diameter tunnel under the Continental Divide. In appreciation for Roberts's efforts, the tunnel, started in 1956 and completed in 1962, was given his name.

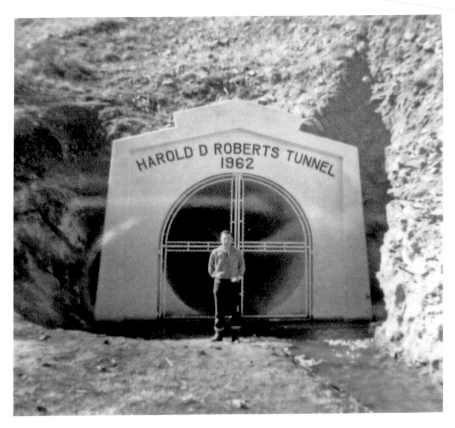

Harold Roberts was instrumental in the creation of this tunnel, which now bears his name and brings Western Slope water to the Denver metro area. *Park County Local History Archives.*

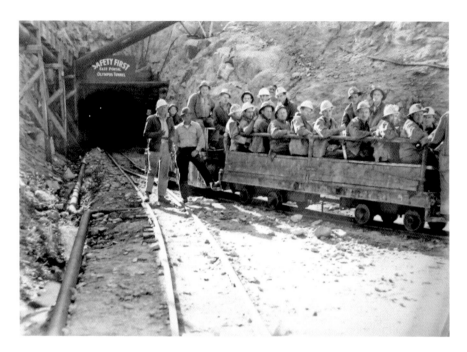

Construction of the Roberts Tunnel was a six-year project bringing lots of jobs to Summit County. Here's one of the work crews, given the task of making a twenty-three-mile-long and ten-foot-diameter hole through the mountains. *Park County Local History Archives.*

ROUTT. This name (rhymes with "mount" and "gout") comes from John Long Routt (1826–1907). Routt, who hailed from Kentucky and Illinois, was Colorado's last territorial governor, from 1875 to 1876, and its first state governor, from 1876 to 1879. An apparent glutton for punishment, Routt, after serving as Denver's mayor from 1883 to 1886, ran for governor a second time, was elected and served as Colorado's seventh state governor, from 1891 to 1893. Somewhere along the way, before his second stint as governor, Routt lost an election for one of Colorado's U.S. Senate seats. A refreshing fact about Routt, unlikely to ever again to be duplicated, is that he won the 1876 gubernatorial election without giving a single public speech. Routt County, in northwest Colorado and now mostly known for the Steamboat Springs ski area, was formed in 1877, during Routt's first term as state governor. Routt County was carved out of Grand County and then, in 1911, lost some of its land to Moffat County.

SECURITY. This name came from a developer, American Builders, selling homes in a new community south of Colorado Springs and wanting its customers to, well, feel safe. Having Fort Carson right next door may also have contributed to the name choice. Security got its start in the mid-1950s. A decade later, Jules Watson formed a company called Widefield Homes and began building and selling homes in the same area. Watson came up with the name Widefield because of the wide-open spaces in this part of El Paso County. Security and Widefield then grew together as adjacent unincorporated communities, under the authority of the government of El Paso County. A shared school district, Widefield District No. 3, serves the area.

SILVERTHORNE. This name, given to a town that started out as a camp for workers constructing Dillon Reservoir, had nothing to do with silver. It came from Marshall Silverthorn, who helped to found Breckenridge (formerly Breckinridge) in 1860. (The *e* at the end of the town's name seems to have come and gone and finally come again and stayed.) Silverthorne is now a thriving community along I-70 and is the second-largest municipality in Summit County, with Breckenridge holding down the top spot. Lots of other places in Colorado did get their name from the metal—Silver Creek (there are eighteen of these), Silver Mountain, Silver Cliff, Silver Plume and Silverton, to name a few.

SPEER. This name comes from Robert Walter Speer (1855–1918), who served two four-year terms in office as Denver's mayor and died halfway through his third term, a victim of an influenza epidemic that swept across the city. Speer was instrumental in pushing through many lasting enhancements to Denver, including the Museum of Nature and Science, an expansion of the Denver Zoo, Denver's mountain parks, much-needed road improvements and the distribution of 110,000 shade trees to city residents. His name lives on with Speer Boulevard, a major artery running along the perimeter of downtown Denver.

STANLEY. This name comes from Freelan Oscar Stanley, who founded the Stanley Motor Carriage Company. That company operated from 1902 to 1924 and is most remembered for passenger vehicles known as Stanley Steamers. Mr. Stanley built the world-famous Stanley Hotel in Estes Park, Colorado, which opened on July 4, 1909, as a destination resort for well-to-do, adventurous tourists. The Stanley Hotel was the inspiration for the Overlook Hotel in Stephen King's novel *The Shining*. (Note to travelers: do not read this book while staying at the hotel.) The hotel proudly promotes itself as being haunted and offers regularly scheduled ghost hunting tours of the facility.

SWEITZER. This name comes from Louis Morgan Sweitzer (1891–1953). Sweitzer was a fruit grower in west-central Colorado who wanted his part of the state to have a water-based recreational site. So, he donated land to the State of Colorado, and that land, in 1960, a few years after his death, became Sweitzer Lake State Park. The centerpiece of the park is a 137-acre reservoir. This reservoir, uniquely, was constructed solely for the purpose of recreation, with no irrigation involved.

TABOR. This name comes from Horace Tabor (1830–1899). Tabor was born in Vermont, spent some time in Kansas and eventually headed west with his wife, Augusta, as a "'59-er" in search of gold. Tabor's first prospecting stop was Buckskin Joe, just west of Alma. Then he went to Leadville, but when gold mining fizzled out there, he returned to Buckskin Joe. However, in 1868, when silver was discovered around Leadville, he returned to that area, where he struck in rich not by reason of prospecting but rather by reason of a grubstake agreement with two guys who discovered one of Leadville's biggest silver strikes, the Little Pittsburg mine. Tabor converted a one-third interest in that mine into other silver mine investments, which proved highly profitable. The Tabors, now wealthy, moved to Denver, where they were generous philanthropists and well connected politically and socially. Horace Tabor served as Colorado's lieutenant governor from 1878 to January 1883, when he was appointed a U.S. senator after Henry Teller resigned his Senate seat to become the United States secretary of the interior. Tabor's stint as senator lasted not quite three months. He then ran unsuccessfully for governor in 1884 and again in 1886 and 1888. Tabor's fortune was wiped out by the 1893 repeal of the Sherman Silver Purchase Act, which tanked the price of silver. His public life ended with service as Denver's postmaster from January 1898 until his death, of appendicitis, in 1899. Tabor is perhaps most famous for divorcing Augusta in 1883 and immediately thereafter marrying his mistress, Elizabeth "Baby Doe" McCourt, a younger woman by some twenty-four years. This chain of events was inspiration for, among other things, a 1956 opera, *The Ballad of Baby Doe*, by American composer Douglas Moore. Tabor's name also lives on with Tabor Peak (13,282 feet), twelve miles to the south of Leadville, and Tabor Lake, a beautiful alpine lake in a cirque tucked into the side of the mountain.

TELLER. This name comes from Henry Moore Teller (1830–1914), who served as a U.S. senator from Colorado from 1876 to 1882 and again from 1885 to 1909. In between his two stints as senator, Teller served as secretary of the interior. In 1896, Teller got cross-wise with other members of the Republican Party and ended up switching sides. He remained a Democrat for the rest of his political career. Teller County was formed in 1899 out of land that was originally the western part of El Paso County. This split-up of El Paso County occurred, at least in part, because the miners living in and around Cripple Creek didn't much like the mine owners, who by and large lived in considerably greater comfort in Colorado Springs.

THATCHER. This name comes from Mahlon D. Thatcher and his slightly less famous brothers, John A. and Henry C. The Thatcher family, centered in Pueblo, had large and profitable interests in banking, ranching and merchandising and were influential in Colorado politics. The Thatcher name shows up frequently in and around Pueblo. There is also a small town in Las Animas County named Thatcher. The town, first organized around 1880 as a stagecoach station, was originally named Hole-in-the-Rock because a spring located there was used to water the horses that pulled the stagecoaches. The name was later changed to honor the accomplishments of Mahlon Thatcher.

THORNTON. This name comes from Daniel Thornton (1911–1976), a Texas cattleman who relocated to Colorado in the early 1940s and who became Colorado's thirty-third governor, serving two consecutive two year terms from 1951 to 1955. Thornton was on a shortlist to be Dwight Eisenhower's running mate when Eisenhower first ran for president. However, he lost out to Richard Nixon (and we know what happened after that). The city of Thornton sits along the I-25 corridor some ten miles north/northeast of downtown Denver and is now Colorado's sixth-largest city, with a population around 120,000. Until 1953, this was farmland, but it was then transformed into a fully planned real estate development.

VAIL. This name—given to a mountain, a town, a pass and the third-largest ski area in North America (after Whistler Blackcomb and Big Sky)—came from Charles Davis Vail. He was the Colorado State Highway commissioner at the time (circa 1940) a route for U.S. Highway 6 (now Interstate 70), traversing Colorado east to west (and vice versa), was chosen and the highway constructed. Vail decided the route over the pass that now bears his name was the best option. Prior to that, Shrine Pass, nearby to the south, was the dominant route over the mountains in this part of Colorado. Now, Shrine Pass is best known for snowmobile and cross-country ski adventures, connecting Vail Pass with the town of Red Cliff. From 1930, when Charles Vail became highway commissioner, through the time of his death in 1945, paved roads in Colorado grew from something like five hundred miles to five thousand miles. Vail Pass rises to 10,667 feet at its summit (placing it nineteenth on the list of Colorado mountain passes served on both sides by a paved road) and is not a good place to be in a blizzard. The Vail Ski Resort opened in 1962. Original investors received a condominium for $10,000 and a lifetime season pass. The town of Vail was incorporated in 1966.

WADSWORTH. This name comes from Benjamin Franklin Wadsworth, who is credited with founding what is now the city of Arvada, Colorado's seventh-most populous city. This founding occurred in 1870, after people in the area decided farming was a more reliable way to earn a living than prospecting. Wadsworth was an energetic promoter of the new community and its first postmaster. Wadsworth Boulevard, a major north–south thoroughfare on the west side of the Denver metropolitan area, is named for Wadsworth.

WALSENBURG. This name comes from Fred Walsen, an early settler who, in 1876, helped to incorporate the city in south-central Colorado (Huerfano County) that bears his name. Walsen ran a general store and was also instrumental in starting the area's the first coal mine. Prior to its incorporation, the community had been known as La Plaza de los Leones, honoring another earlier settler, Don Miguel Antonio León. (Walsenburg is easier to remember.) After the city's incorporation, postal authorities tried to change the name one more time (to Tourist City), but the town's citizens, not wanting their community to have the tackiest name in the state, demanded a return of the Walsenburg name. In the late 1800s and early 1900s, Walsenburg grew into an important coal mining hub. Some 500 million tons of coals were mined in the area before various market forces shut down the industry. Walsenburg is also famous (sort of) as the home of Robert Ford, a saloonkeeper credited with assassinating outlaw Jesse James. The house where Ford lived during his saloonkeeper/outlaw assassin days still stands, at 320 West Seventh Street.

WELD. This name has been given to various places in Colorado in honor of Lewis Ledyard Weld (1833–1865). Weld, born in Connecticut to a prominent East Coast family, was a member of the Yale University class of 1854. He worked his way west for various reasons and ended up practicing law in the Colorado Territory. Although Weld was only twenty-eight years old at the time, President Lincoln, in 1861, appointed him as secretary of the Colorado Territory; shortly thereafter, he became the acting governor of the territory. He held that position until April 1862, when he resigned to join the Union army. He rose to the rank of lieutenant colonel before he became ill. He died at a military hospital in January 1865. Weld County, in north-central Colorado, was named for Colonel Weld when it was formed in 1861 as one of the original seventeen counties making up the Colorado Territory. Over the years, Weld County lost land to Washington, Logan, Morgan, Yuma, Phillips and Sedgwick Counties. In 1955, Weld County was the scene of a gruesome and tragic airplane crash. United Airlines Flight 629, bound for Portland from Denver, exploded in midair, killing all forty-four people on board. The explosion was caused by a time bomb placed by a man named John Graham in the luggage of his mother, who was a passenger on the plane. Graham was executed for his crime in 1957.

WESTMINSTER. This name, in an indirect way, comes to Colorado from Westminster Abbey and Westminster Palace, two structures of great historical and religious significance in London. (The United Kingdom Parliament meets in Westminster Palace.) The Colorado city of Westminster, north of Denver, got its name because a man named Henry Mayham came there from New York in the late 1800s and started a Presbyterian college he called Westminster University. Mayham's goal was to make this the "Princeton of the West," but that never happened. Mayham's university didn't admit women, and most of the men who might have attended went off to fight World War I and never came back. So, Westminster University, due to a lack of students (and therefore a lack of funds), shut down in 1917. What came of Mayham's efforts of more lasting significance is a tall, striking building, constructed of red sandstone, at the highest point in Adams County. The building still stands at the intersection of Eighty-Third Avenue and Federal Boulevard and has been known as Westminster Castle and, more dramatically, the Pillar of Fire. The building is now owned by the Pillar of Fire Church, which conducts various educational activities at the site. Before acquiring the name Westminster, which occurred at the time of the city's incorporation in 1911, it had been known as Harris, after a real estate developer by that name from Connecticut. And before that, it was known as DeSpain Junction, after an early settler named Pleasant DeSpain.

WIDEFIELD. This name came from Jules Watson, who called his homebuilding company Widefield Homes. This was an appropriate name for use in a part of

El Paso County, south of Colorado Springs and just east of the I-25 corridor, where sagebrush is the predominant vegetative life form. Widefield Homes focused its business on an area first developed by another homebuilding company, American Builders. American Builders, wanting people who were thinking about buying its homes to feel safe, named its development Security. Security and Widefield eventually grew together as adjacent unincorporated communities, under the authority of the government of El Paso County. They jointly share at least one form of government, a school district: Widefield District No. 3.

WINDOM. This name comes to Colorado from William Windom (1829–1891). Windom was a congressman and senator from Minnesota and served on two occasions as secretary of the treasury. In 1880, Windom sought the Republican nomination for president, but he didn't get very far, receiving only ten votes on the first ballot. If you're a numismatist, you might already know that William Windom's picture appears on the two-dollar U.S. silver certificate that was in circulation from 1891 to 1896. In 1902, the U.S. Geological Survey, while exploring and mapping the rugged Needle Mountains in southwest Colorado, named Windom Peak in his honor. Windom Peak, at 14,082 feet, holds thirty-third place on the highest Colorado mountains list.

WYNKOOP. This name comes from Edward Wanshear Wynkoop (1836–1891), credited with being one of the founders of the city of Denver. Wynkoop was a Union army officer from Colorado during the Civil War. He gained modest fame for his investigation of the conduct of Colonel John Chivington at the Sand Creek Massacre. That investigation led to strident (and well-deserved) criticism of Chivington and his troops. Wynkoop later became a federal Indian agent for the Southern Cheyenne and Arapahoe tribes and was a vocal proponent of peace with the Indians. When a Cheyenne Indian village in Oklahoma was destroyed by the U.S. Cavalry in 1868, he resigned his position in protest. After that, he ended up as warden of the New Mexico State Penitentiary, and at the time of his death, his home was in Santa Fe. Wynkoop's name lives on with, among other things, Wynkoop Street in Lo-Do and the Wynkoop Brewing Company, a brewpub and restaurant business started by Colorado's forty-second governor, John Hickenlooper, and others.

CHAPTER 7

FARMERS, RANCHERS, PIONEERS AND SETTLERS

It didn't take long for people to realize that prospectors had to eat, and agricultural activity in Colorado started to gain momentum in tandem with the 1859 Pikes Peak gold rush. However, the area's high altitude and modest precipitation created serious challenges. Plus, agriculture in Colorado got off to a bad start because of Stephen Long's famous statement, made back in the 1820s, to the effect that eastern Colorado, as well as western Kansas and Nebraska, was a great big desert. Nonetheless, irrigation made land close to the mountains productive, and creative early settlers and legislators, after some false starts, worked out rules to allow irrigation to occur and its benefits to be shared in a reasonable fashion.

Dry land farming in the eastern plains of Colorado was more problematic. During wet years, farming was kind to settlers accustomed to the precipitation they had experienced farther east, and aggressive promotion and the Homestead Act of 1862 brought them to the Colorado prairies by the thousands. But when the dry years came, crops would wither and die, and dust was the only commodity in abundance. Then settlers would, again in droves, pack up and head back to wherever they had come from. Eventually, innovations from agricultural science—and sugar beets—brought sustainable life to the prairies, and in a few cases (for example, Charles Boettcher and his son, Claude), great fortunes were made from agriculture. Nonetheless, boom and bust, in the tradition of prospecting and mining, was the norm for those seeking to earn a living by growing things out on the prairies.

As for ranching, cattlemen coming north from Texas and New Mexico in the 1860s found that raising cattle in Colorado could be very profitable. This was so because the cattle could eat grass on public lands at little or no cost. And cattle in Colorado, as elsewhere, had an innate ability to increase herd size without much encouragement from owners. Raising cattle in Colorado was so profitable that by the 1870s, it had gone corporate. For example, the Prairie Cattle Company was running six thousand head by 1878 and paying 20 percent dividends to its shareholders. Again in keeping with Colorado's boom-and-bust tradition, however, growing and selling cattle took a hit in the 1880s due to drought, severe winters and oversupply. This led to a ten-year decline in cattle prices and many soured investments.

In the 1870s, Colorado also experienced some innovative efforts at what could be considered agricultural socialism. Of particular note was the Union Colony, a utopian agricultural community backed by Horace Greeley and promoted by Greeley in his *New York Tribune* newspaper. The boots-on-the-ground guy who organized and managed the Union Colony was the *Tribune's* agricultural editor, Nathan Meeker (later to gain fame when, in 1879, he was gruesomely murdered by a small group of Ute Indians during the Meeker Massacre). The Union Colony brought together seven hundred settlers thought to be of high moral character and supporters of the temperance movement, chosen out of an applicant pool of three thousand. Irrigation was a shared resource for the community, and in its early years, the Union Colony thrived and generated imitators. But differences of opinion and beliefs soon unraveled the structure, leaving Meeker substantially in debt and causing the Union Colony to evolve into the more traditional city of Greeley (although Greeley retained a ban on alcohol until 1972).

Just as farming and ranching was of great importance to the settlement of Colorado, and had a substantial influence on the naming of places, so, too, with pioneers and settlers who found employment, or entrepreneurial opportunity, outside of agriculture. These hardy folks built communities, invited friends and family to come west and join them and gave their communities names, often imported from where they had come from.

In this mix, the United States Post Office also needs brief mention. Starting with the Pikes Peak gold rush of 1859 and accelerating with the coming of the railroads, towns began popping up all over the place in Colorado, and a priority for town organizers was the establishment of an official U.S. Post Office. This required an application to a Washington, D.C.–based bureaucracy that, by 1841, already had fourteen thousand employees and, by 1869, was tending to the affairs of twenty-seven thousand local post offices. Up until 1872, the United States Post Office was a sub-cabinet-level department of the federal government. In 1872, however, it was elevated to a cabinet-level agency. (A century later, in 1971, it was given a new name—the United States Postal Service—and demoted to an independent agency expected, financially at least, to fend for itself.) Until the Pendleton Civil Service Reform Act of 1883, positions within the post office were obtained by political patronage, and competence to carry out the agency's mission was largely irrelevant. This may explain why community names in Colorado occasionally suffered a mutation during the post office application process. Rather than seeking redress from the bureaucracy, communities often just accepted the surprise name given them in response to their post office application.

In all events, the United States Post Office was important to the development of the West, including Colorado. Notwithstanding its flaws, the postal service facilitated commerce and westward migration in multiple ways. An occasional name aberration was a small price to pay for the benefit provided.

—•—

ABARR. Abarr was the maiden name of Ethel R. Hoffman, the postmistress of a town in far eastern Colorado (Yuma County) originally called Brownsville. The name was changed to Abarr in 1924 because Colorado already had a town named Brownsville, and since zip codes hadn't been invented yet, this two-towns-with-the-same-name situation was giving the U.S. Post Office fits. Mrs. Hoffman most likely came to her job as postmistress because her husband, S.E. Hoffman, a local store owner, was instrumental in surveying, platting and recording the Abarr town site.

AGUILAR. This name comes from José Ramón Aguilar (1852–1929), a prominent pioneer and early farmer, rancher and politician in south-central Colorado. He was one of the founders of the town, along the Apishapa River in Las Animas County, that bears his name. Among his other accomplishments, Aguilar, although busy running a successful cattle, sheep and farming operation, found time to serve as a state representative, county commissioner, mayor and school board member.

ALMONT. This name comes to Colorado thanks to a Kentucky racehorse named Almont, famous in its time. Sam Fisher, a prominent early Gunnison County rancher, purchased a stallion sired by Almont, of which he was justly proud. When the time came in the early 1880s to give a name to a town where the East River and the Taylor River come together to form the Gunnison River, Almont was chosen as the name.

ARCHULETA. This name comes into Colorado history because of J.M. Archuleta, who was head of one of the old Spanish families living in New Mexico. A county in southwest Colorado was named after him in 1885. It seems that the Archuleta clan, although mostly resident in New Mexico, nonetheless controlled the politics of the new Colorado county. This situation led to an armed conflict with the "American" residents of the county a few years after the county was first created and named. Apparently, the New Mexicans prevailed since the name of the county survived.

AULT. This name comes from Alexander Ault. In 1897, Ault's name was given to a town in Weld County in appreciation for his actions that saved many local farmers from bankruptcy. Alexander Ault, it seems, was a wheat merchant from nearby Fort Collins, and during times when the market for wheat tanked and before there were grain storage elevators, he would purchase the crops of these farmers when no one else would. The town, which grew up along the tracks of a Union Pacific rail line running north to Wyoming, was originally named High Land and then Burgdorff Siding (for some local railroad guy named Burgdorff) before the name was changed to Ault.

AVON. This name derives from the Avon River in England and, in the 1880s, was given to a town along the Eagle River (and now along I-70) by a settler from England who apparently thought the town needed some old-world charm. Avon is best known these days as the gateway to the upscale Beaver Creek Ski Resort, which borders the town on its south side.

AVONDALE. This name comes from the English town of Stratford-upon-Avon, famous as the birthplace of William Shakespeare. A pioneering local merchant, Sam Taylor, was from Stratford-upon-Avon, and sometime around 1890, he came up with the Avondale name for this town site. Previously, it had been known as Forest Park. Avondale (what there is of it) is in Pueblo County, east of the city of Pueblo, along the Arkansas River.

BACA. This name comes from Felipe Baca, a well-respected pioneer, rancher and territorial legislator. In 1889, a county in the far southeast corner of Colorado was named in his honor. Baca also left his mark in Trinidad, Colorado, located in Las Animas County to the west of Baca County, where a house he once lived in (purchased with his wife, Dolores, for twenty-two thousand pounds of wool) has been preserved and is now a state historical site open to the public.

BAILEY. This name comes from William Bailey, a settler who, in 1864, established a hotel and stagecoach station at the site of the town in Park County along U.S. Highway 285 that bears his name. The town was originally named Bailey's Ranch but was later shortened to just Bailey. In 1878, the Denver, South Park and Pacific Railroad, a narrow-gauge operation, established a terminal at Bailey.

BAXTER. There are at least three Baxters whose name was given to a Colorado location. Oliver H.P. Baxter, a pioneering rancher, owned the land that became the small town of Baxter. This town is east of Pueblo along U.S. Highway 50. Oliver served in the Colorado territorial legislature during the 1860s. Then, on the other side of the state in Garfield County, we have Baxter Pass (8,422 feet), named after C.O. Baxter, the engineer who managed to build a railroad across this route. Finally, we have Baxterville, a small enclave within the town of South Fork, Colorado. South Fork borders the Rio Grande in Rio Grande County, at the east end of Wolf Creek Pass. The Baxter of Baxterville—first name unknown—apparently owned a restaurant in the area that was famous for its chili.

BAYFIELD. This name comes from William A. Bay. In 1898, Bay donated eighty acres of land he owned along the Los Pinos River in La Plata County for a town site. A man named Schiller also donated eighty acres of land for this town site. Bay and Schiller then flipped a coin to see who would have the right to name the town. Bay won, and he named the town Bayfield. We'll never know what the town name would be if Schiller had won. Schillerfield? Schillerton? Schillerville? Or perhaps Los Pinos, which was the name used for the town prior to the Bay/Schiller coin toss.

BEULAH. This name comes from a Hebrew word meaning "married" or "inhabited." The name shows up in the Bible (Isaiah 62:4) in vague reference to a blessed land that was off in the future somewhere. It also appears in John

Bunyan's *Pilgrim's Progress.* An upscale community in the foothills west of Pueblo chose the name Beulah to replace the community's previous name, Mace's Hole. That name came from Juan Mace, a legendary outlaw who was big on rustling cattle and stealing horses and who had made this area his headquarters. Beulah won out in a name election contest over Silver Glen, which finished a close second.

BOONE. This name comes to Colorado (sort of) by way of legendary Kentucky mountain man Daniel Boone. The small town of Boone, in Pueblo County, is named for Colonel Albert Gallatin Boone, who was one of Daniel Boone's grandsons. Colonel Boone was also the town's founder and first postmaster, as well as an accomplished trapper, trader and Indian negotiator in his own right. When the town was first laid out in the early 1860s, it was known as Booneville or Boonetown. The name was later shortened to just Boone. Boone is some twenty-one miles due east of Pueblo along Colorado Highway 96 and the Arkansas River.

BRIGHTON. This name came to Colorado because Alice Carmichael, wife of the man (Daniel Carmichael) who, in 1881, filed the first plat for the town of Brighton, wanted her Colorado hometown to honor the name of her back east hometown, Brighton Beach, New York. Daniel told Alice she could name the town, and she chose Brighton. When the town was first created in 1870 as a railroad depot (population seven), it was named Hughes Station, after Bela Hughes, then president of the Union Pacific Railroad. Brighton (current population more than thirty-six thousand and now a city) is north and east of Denver and is the county seat of Adams County.

BRUSH. Although Colorado has an abundance of various types of vegetation that could be called "brush" (and at least thirteen streams named for the stuff), the community of Brush, in northeast Colorado (Morgan County), was named after a pioneering rancher in the area, Jared L. Brush. Jared Brush ended up serving as Colorado's lieutenant governor for two terms, from 1895 to 1899. He lived in Greeley, and never in Brush, but he apparently liked to visit the place and did so at every opportunity. Brush was incorporated as a statutory city in 1884.

BURLINGTON. The town of Burlington, county seat for Kit Carson County in far east-central Colorado, got its name because early residents of the town came from Burlington, Kansas, and Burlington, Iowa, and apparently liked the name. In 1887, a man named Lowell laid out a town in a place where he thought the Chicago, Rock Island and Pacific Railroad was going to lay its tracks and establish a depot. But Lowell got the location wrong, and when the railroad did come, a year later, it put its depot a mile or so to the east. The town site Lowell had platted was then abandoned, and the people living there packed up and moved to what is now Burlington, choosing that name for the relocated town.

CAMERON. This name comes from Civil War veteran (on the Union army side) General Robert A. Cameron. He was the founder, in 1872, of something called the Fort Collins Agricultural Colony. This was essentially a land development adjacent to the fledgling town of Fort Collins, and its three thousand acres were eventually absorbed into the city limits of Fort Collins. The goal of the colony was to bring additional settlers and diversified economic activity, including agricultural activity, to the Fort Collins area. Lots in the colony of various sizes (ten, twenty and forty acres) were established and made available, by drawing and payment of a modest price, to anyone "possessed of good moral character." (I have found no reference as to how this was measured.) General Cameron's name lives on with Cameron Pass, which has a paved road rising to 10,230 feet, connecting Fort Collins on the east to Walden on the west via Colorado Highway 14. Cameron Pass lies roughly three miles to the north of the northern boundary of Rocky Mountain National Park, in north-central Colorado.

CARBONDALE. Although coal was mined up until 1991 in the Crystal River Valley to the east of the town of Carbondale, the town (incorporated in 1888) actually got its name from Carbondale, Pennsylvania, the former home of a large number of the town's earliest settlers. Despite the mining activity going on all around it at the time of its formation, Carbondale was primarily an agricultural community, the idea being that growing food and selling it to miners was more likely to produce a steady income than was mining. Until the Idaho potato industry took off in the early twentieth century, Carbondale was famous for its potatoes; should you happen to be a connoisseur of potatoes, you might want to attend the town's annual Potato Day festival. Carbondale is to the north of Aspen and the south of Glenwood Springs, in the Roaring Fork River Valley. The mega-inflation in housing prices in and around Aspen has gone down valley far enough to cause Carbondale to be a hotbed for pricey vacation homes.

CENTENNIAL. Colorado is known as the Centennial State because it became a state in 1876, the centennial of the American Revolution. The city of Centennial, which is in Arapahoe County to the east of I-25 and a part of the sprawl generally thought of as Denver, was incorporated in 2001. With a population of some 100,000, this was at the time (and might still be) the largest municipal incorporation in the history of the United States. When the voters in this area approved the incorporation, they also approved the name Centennial. Centennial has a busy airport, used by private and business aircraft, and more importantly, the city is right next door to the Denver Broncos' training complex.

CORDOVA. This name comes from José de Jesús Córdova (1856–1929). Cordova was a well-known, longtime rancher in south-central Colorado who served for three terms as a Las Animas County commissioner. Cordova Pass was named in his honor in 1935. (Córdova had been instrumental in causing a road to be built over the pass.) Cordova Pass sits along the west shoulder of West Spanish Peak, climbs to 11,248 feet and is served by a gravel road accessible by a normal passenger vehicle, although the road is usually shut down by snow from mid-November to late May. Prior to completion of the road, the pass had been known as Apishapa Pass. Since *apishapa* is an Arapahoe Indian word possibly meaning "stinking water," the Las Animas County tourist and convention bureau probably decided that Cordova Pass would be a better name.

COTOPAXI. This name comes to Colorado by way of a 19,347-foot volcano in Ecuador. Although no volcanoes (at least active ones) exist in the area, a town along the Arkansas River between Cañon City and Salida was given this name in the 1870s by Emanuel Saltiel, who owned a nearby mine. Saltiel, in 1882, tried to start a Jewish agricultural settlement here on land he owned, and he invited Russian and Polish Jewish immigrants to come to Cotopaxi as part of this project. However, the immigrants didn't stay long, apparently concluding that Saltiel's representations about what they would find in Cotopaxi were not entirely consistent with reality. Cotopaxi is a frequent stopping point for fishermen looking for Arkansas River fishing reports. These reports, in the tradition of Mr. Saltiel, are also not always consistent with reality.

CROWLEY. The Crowley name came from John H. Crowley, who was a state senator from the area that became Crowley County in 1911. Crowley

County, on the eastern plains of Colorado, was carved out of a part of Otero County. Otero County had, in turn, originally been a part of Bent County. At one time, Crowley County was a lush farming area, irrigated by water from the Arkansas River transported over a considerable distance by means of a canal. However, the rights to this water have, in large part, been acquired by fast-growing front-range cities, causing the land in Crowley County to revert back to ranching, which needs less water than farming. Crowley County is unique in that, at least as of the 2010 census, 46 percent of its residents were prisoners in a prison located there.

De Beque. This name comes from Dr. Wallace A.E. de Beque. Dr. De Beque, a transplant from Fairplay, gave his family name to a town he founded in the west-central part of the state (Mesa County) in the early 1880s. But then Henry Collbran, a railroad executive with the Colorado Midland Railway, came along and wanted to change the name of the town to Collbran. Dr. De Beque objected to this, leading to a spirited debate and a bizarre political compromise whereby the residents of the nearby town of Hawxhurst (thirty-five miles to the southeast) agreed to change the name of their town to Collbran, thereby allowing the town of De Beque to retain its name. These two towns, both in Mesa County, are to the east of Grand Junction.

Dunckley. This name comes from a family of early-day ranchers in north-central Colorado consisting of Bob, Richard, Tom, George and John Dunckley. That was enough of a presence to earn a town name in Routt County and a mountain pass name (9,763 feet) in Rio Blanco County. The town, south and west of Steamboat Springs and north of the Flat Tops Wilderness, is now a ghost town. The pass, near Yampa, Colorado, remains and is served by a gravel road with no winter maintenance.

Eaton. This name comes from Benjamin Harrison Eaton (1833–1904). Eaton is given credit for bringing irrigation water to what is now Weld County and vicinity, thereby causing previously dry prairie terrain to blossom into highly productive farmland (and also planting the seeds for multiple later legal fights over water ownership). Eaton was Colorado's fourth governor, from 1885 to 1887, and was known as the "farmer governor." The town of Eaton is some eight miles north of Greeley, along U.S. Highway 85.

Englewood. This name came to Colorado from Englewood, Illinois (or possibly Englewood, New Jersey), in keeping with the seemingly popular custom of naming new cities after old cities where residents used to live. The city of Englewood, incorporated in 1903, is tucked into an area to the south and west of Denver and has a current population of some thirty-one thousand residents. Once upon a time, it was the home of the largest indoor shopping mall west of the Mississippi, called Cinderella City. But Cinderella City became old and out of date, and it was scrapped in 1999.

GARDEN. This name, of course, comes from gardens, and since Greeley had lots of them, it decided to market itself as the Garden City of the West. Then, shortly after Prohibition ended, the voters in Greeley decided in 1935 to keep it a dry city, meaning no liquor could be sold or manufactured there. One consequence of this was the founding of the town of Garden City, right next door to Greeley, where the citizens of Greeley could visit and buy alcohol. Although Greeley is no longer dry, Garden City survives as a statutory town. However, it is now entirely surrounded by Greeley and another town, Evans, and the children living in Garden City go to school in Greeley.

GARO. This name comes from Marie and Adolf Guiraud, pioneering sheep ranchers in an area between Fairplay and Hartsel. Since very few people in the area spoke French or knew how to spell French names, Garo was as close as they could come when the time came to name a town honoring the couple. Garo is now a ghost town, and little of it remains.

GEORGE. This name makes it onto our list thanks to two guys named, well, George—George Frost and George Griffith to be exact. George Frost was a pioneer rancher who, probably without any legal right to do so, built a dam across the South Platte River as it comes out of Eleven Mile Canyon in Park County. This dam resulted in a lake, which became known as George's Lake. Later, when a post office was established in 1891 for a community next to the lake, the name given the community was Lake George. In the winter, George Frost would harvest ice from the lake and sell it to the Colorado Midland Railway, which he no doubt found more profitable than ranching. However, the railroad pulled out of the area in 1918, ending the ice business. The town and the lake have lived on, largely as a vacation home community. As for the other George, George Griffith, he, together with his brother, David— both prospectors from Kentucky—founded the municipality of Georgetown in 1859. Georgetown, along the I-70 corridor east a bit from the Eisenhower Tunnel and Loveland Ski Area, is now the county seat of Clear Creek

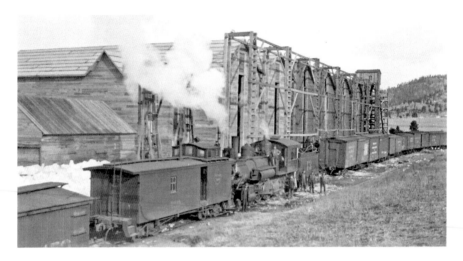

The Lake George ice factory, which provided ice to the Colorado Midland Railway while it lasted. *Park County Local History Archives.*

County. It was a commercial center for silver mining activity in Colorado before silver mining went bust. Georgetown has the distinction of being the only municipality in Colorado that still functions under a charter granted by the Colorado Territory, before Colorado became a state. Under this charter, the town council is referred to as the "board of selectmen," and the person who acts as mayor is called the "police judge."

Glenwood. This name came to Colorado from Glenwood, Iowa, because a couple of the first settlers in what is now Glenwood Springs were from there, didn't much like the name originally given to the town (Defiance) and were probably homesick for a place that didn't consist mostly of bars and brothels. The "Springs" part of the Glenwood Springs name refers to the hot springs in the area, which continue to serve as a major tourist draw. Glenwood Springs sits at the confluence of the Roaring Fork River and the Colorado River, was first established in 1883 and is the county seat for Garfield County. Of modest note on the trivia front is the fact that Glenwood Springs was one of the first places in the country to have electric lights.

Hardscrabble. Legend has it that this name came about when a group of early Colorado settlers, being pursued by Indians, had to go up a steep creek drainage to avoid losing their scalps. They later described their escape route as a "hard scramble," leading to the creek being named Hardscrabble Creek. Colorado now also has Hardscrabble Pass, which crosses the Wet Mountains connecting Wetmore on the east and Westcliffe on the west. The paved road over Hardscrabble Pass, topping out at 9,085 feet, is Colorado Highway 96. This road has been designated the Frontier Pathways Scenic and Historic Byway. The view of the Wetmore Valley that you see from this pass, as well as that of the Sangre de Cristo Range on the valley's west side, is stunning.

HILLROSE. This name came from Rose Hill, who was either the sister or the daughter of Kate Emerson. Emerson, in the early 1900s, deeded the land for a town site in Morgan County being established by the Lincoln Land Company, an affiliate of the Burlington Railroad. She was given the right to name the town, and she chose Hillrose by reversing her sister's (or her daughter's) first and last name.

HOLLY. This name comes from Hiram S. Holly, who, along with 1,300 head of cattle, settled in an area four miles west of the Colorado/Kansas line in 1871. The town of Holly, in Prowers County, has the distinction of having the lowest elevation—at 3,392 feet—of any town in Colorado. The Holly Sugar Corporation had its start there in 1905. That corporation was acquired by Imperial Sugar Company in 1988. Imperial, a public company headquartered in Sugar Land, Texas, ended up in a Chapter 11 bankruptcy proceeding in 2001. It survived bankruptcy and was taken private by a commodities investor in 2012. People in Colorado Springs still refer to one of the city's major downtown office buildings as the Holly Sugar Building even though the Holly Sugar name was taken off the building many years ago.

HOLYOKE. This name comes from Holyoke, Massachusetts, and was given to a town in far northeastern Colorado (Phillips County) in 1887 or thereabouts. Holyoke, Massachusetts, was in turn named for Reverend Edward Holyoke, who was the ninth president of Harvard College, holding that office from 1737 to 1769. This was a remarkable accomplishment since, upon his graduation from Harvard in 1705 at age sixteen, Holyoke had set the college's record for black marks and fines resulting from disciplinary violations.

HOOSIER. Various places in Colorado are named "hoosier" thanks to people (mostly prospectors) coming to Colorado from Indiana, the Hoosier State. This includes Hoosier Pass, which crosses the Continental Divide and connects the Breckenridge/Lake Dillon area on the north with South Park on the south. Hoosier Pass rises to 11,541 feet, putting it in ninth place on the list of Colorado mountain passes served by an

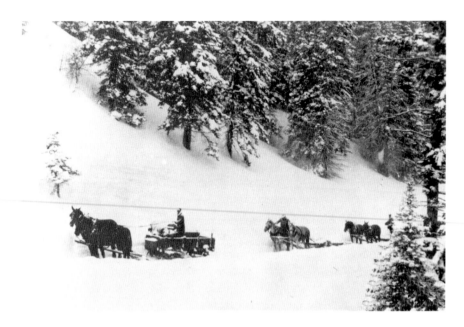

A winter crossing of Hoosier Pass before the invention of SUVs. *Park County Local History Archives.*

improved road. (If you exclude the high point along Trail Ridge Road from the list, Hoosier Pass moves up to eighth place.) There is actually a second, less well-known, Hoosier Pass in Teller County near Cripple Creek. This one only makes it to 10,313 feet. Perhaps of greater interest here is the derivation of the name "Hoosier." Historians in Indiana (and who should know this) believe the name originated somewhere in the southern states—Virginia, the Carolinas or Tennessee—and referred to a backwoodsman or a rough countryman. A less flattering meaning associated with the name is "country bumpkin."

KENOSHA. This name comes to Colorado from Kenosha, Wisconsin. That's because a man who regularly drove a stagecoach across what is now Kenosha Pass was from there and decided to name the pass after his hometown. Kenosha Pass is (and has been for a long, long time) a major route between Denver on the east and Fairplay on the west. The pass rises to 10,001 feet and provides striking views of several of Colorado's mountain subranges and fourteeners, as well as the vast expanse of South Park. It is crossed by U.S. Highway 285. As for Kenosha, Wisconsin, its name came from Kenozia, a name given to the area by early Native Americans. When settlers from the east arrived and shooed the Indians out, they changed the name first to Pike

150

Creek and then to Southport. The name was changed one more time, to Kenosha, in 1850, and this time the name stuck.

KIM. This name comes from a 1901 Rudyard Kipling novel by that name. The residents of a small town in far southeast Colorado (Las Animas County), who were apparently well read, chose this name for their community. At the time the name choosing occurred, the other option being considered was Dexter, the middle name of the town's founder. However, Kim won out.

LOCHBUIE. This name (pronounced lok-*boo*-ee) comes from a settlement on the Isle of Mull in Scotland. It was given to a town in north-central Colorado (Weld County) in 1974 when the town was incorporated. The town was established in the 1960s as part of a real estate development called the Spacious Living Mobile Home Park, which soon became known as Space City, with the reference to "space" coming from the wide-open spaces in this part of Colorado rather than outer space. Apparently, one of the founders of this community came from the Isle of Mull and wanted a touch of home to be included in his new address, so Space City gave way to Lochbuie.

MANASSA. This name comes from Manasseh, who, in the Bible, was the eldest son of Joseph. The name Manassa was given to a town in south-central Colorado (Conejos County) in 1879 by Mormon pioneers who settled in the area. Manassa has gotten lots of mileage out of having been the hometown of Jack Dempsey, world heavyweight boxing champion from 1919 to 1926, who was known as the Manassa Mauler.

McCLURE. This name comes from Thomas McClure, an Irish mining immigrant who, when not busy trying to strike it rich through mining, developed a variety of potato known as the Red McClure. Red McClure potatoes grew very well in the area around Carbondale, Colorado, and in the early twentieth century (before Carbondale became a site for overpriced homes purchased by people who couldn't afford even more overpriced homes in Aspen), Carbondale's potato production exceeded that of the entire state of Idaho. McClure Pass (8,755 feet) lies along paved Colorado Highway 133 and connects Carbondale on the east with Paonia on the west.

MEAD. This name comes from Dr. Martin Luther Mead, one of the first medical doctors—and an early homesteader—in the area where the town of Mead, in Weld County, is now located. The town was platted in 1905 by Dr. Mead's son, Paul Mead, who named the town after his father. The inspiration for the town was a spur railroad line constructed to ship sugar beets grown in the area to processing plants to the north.

Montrose. Demonstrating that at least some of the people giving names to Colorado places more than a century ago were well read, the name Montrose comes from a novel by Sir Walter Scott published in 1819, *A Legend of Montrose*. This novel mostly dealt with a steamy love triangle wherein two male suitors were in testosterone-enhanced pursuit of a woman named Annot Lyle. But the background noise for the story had to do with a civil war in Scotland in the 1640s wherein the Earl of Montrose played a prominent role. The city of Montrose was chartered in 1882, and Montrose County, in west-central Colorado, was created shortly thereafter in 1883.

Nathrop. Nathrop is a small town along the Arkansas River and U.S. Highway 285, south of Buena Vista, in Chaffee County. It was originally named Chalk Creek, for the creek by that name that comes out of the mountains to the west and empties into the Arkansas River near the town. The current name for the town is an adaptation of the name of a pioneer merchant in the area, Charles Nachtrieb, who owned some of the land that became the town site. (Apparently, no one wanted to live in a town named Nachtrieb.) Nachtrieb didn't get to enjoy living in the town named after him for very long. He was murdered there in 1881, in his own store by an angry cowhand, soon after the town was established.

Nucla. This name, given to a small town in far southwest Colorado (Montrose County) and not far from Naturita, comes from the word *nucleus*. The town was founded in 1894 by a group of socialists, doing business as the Colorado Co-Operative Company. These folks were convinced that their model for a community, based on the principle of sharing, would spread throughout the world and that Nucla would become the center—the nucleus—for the movement. This, of course, never happened. However, the name turned out to be forward-looking when uranium was discovered in the area and mined, leading to an association of the town name with the word *nuclear*. Nucla made news back in May 2013 when the town board passed what it called the "Family Protection Order." This ordinance required all heads of a household, with certain limited exceptions (such as convicted felons), to own a gun. Since just about everyone in Nucla already owned a gun (usually several), not much changed following the passage of the ordinance.

OLATHE. This name came to Colorado from a similarly named town in Kansas. The Colorado town, along U.S. Highway 50 in Montrose County, was originally named Brown and then Colorow. Town residents later realized that Colorow was the name of one of the renegade Ute Indians involved in the Meeker Massacre, and they decided a name change was in order. Olathe apparently comes from an expression in the Shawnee Indian language meaning "fine" or "beautiful." The highlight of the year in Olathe is the annual Sweet Corn Festival, held the first Saturday in August. Motels in the area book up early, so plan accordingly.

PARKER. This name comes from James S. Parker, who served as postmaster for a settlement in Douglas County that now bears his name on the southeastern fringe of the Denver metropolitan area. In the beginning (1870s), this was a dusty little station on the stagecoach line between Denver and Colorado Springs called Pine Grove. Although Parker now has a population of about fifty thousand, it still calls itself a "town." The only Colorado "town" bigger than Parker is nearby Castle Rock, with a population estimated at fifty-five thousand. (Ouray, on the other hand, with a population of one thousand, is chartered as a city.)

PEARL. This name comes to Colorado from H. Pearl Hartt, whose claim to fame is mostly that she married John Kelly Hartt, who was a big-time pioneering sheep rancher in north-central Colorado and south-central Wyoming. Mrs. Hartt's status as the wife of a wealthy rancher led to the naming of Pearl Lake, in Routt County, north of Steamboat Springs, and later to the naming of Pearl Lake State Park. After her husband's death, Mrs. Hartt sold the family ranch land to the U.S. Forest Service. This sale helped outdoor recreation to supplant agriculture as the primary economic activity in this part of Colorado.

PISGAH. This name comes from a mountain east of the Dead Sea from which Moses claimed to have seen the promised land shortly before his death, thereby completing his mission. Settlers moving west and hoping to find their own promised land gave this name to numerous places. In Colorado, there are three smallish mountains using the Pisgah name. The highest of these is in Clear Creek County and has a summit elevation of a mere 10,081 feet. There is also a well-known Mount Pisgah near Cripple Creek, site of one of the more famous mine salting frauds in Colorado history.

PROWERS. We can thank John Wesley Prowers (1838–1884) for the frequent use of this name in southeast Colorado. Prowers first came to Colorado from Missouri in 1856 at the age of eighteen. He worked in and around Bent's Fort in various jobs associated with Indian trading commerce. This included heading up wagon trains of merchandise coming from the Midwest to Bent's Fort, perilous assignments that he managed to survive. Prowers eventually settled down in southeast Colorado and became a wealthy cattleman, at one time having a herd of some ten thousand animals. In 1863, he married Amache, otherwise known as Amy. Amy was the daughter of a Cheyenne Indian chief named Ochanee, which means "one-eye" in the Cheyenne language. Ochanee was killed during the Sand Creek Massacre. Legend has it he could have escaped that day but chose to stay—and die—with his people. Prowers served as a county commissioner in Bent County and a representative to the Colorado legislature from that area. Prowers County, in far southeast Colorado and a split-off from Bent County, was named in his honor in 1889, five years after his death. In this part of the state, only the signs along the road (and the color of the highway patrol cars) let you know when you're leaving Colorado and entering Kansas.

RAMAH. This name comes from a city in ancient Israel referenced several times in the Bible and where bad things regularly happened to good people. The name was given to a town in El Paso County roughly forty miles east of Colorado Springs established in the 1880s by the El Paso Land and Water Company. Ramah was a thriving place until the Rock Island Railroad pulled out in the mid-1900s. Now, its population is less than two hundred, and the name is rarely heard, except when a tornado passes through the neighborhood.

RANGELY. This name comes from Rangeley, Maine, the hometown of one of the original settlers in what is now Rangely, Colorado. (The change in spelling from Rangeley to Rangely may have been accidental. Early settlers in Colorado, like post office employees, weren't always the best spellers.) This town, in far northwest Colorado (Rio Blanco County), is some thirteen miles from the Utah border (as the buzzard flies). It started life as an Indian trading post before the Ute Indians were herded off to reservations in the Four Corners region, mostly in Utah. Rangely's reason for being eventually morphed into oil and natural gas drilling, which continues to be the economic lifeblood of Rio Blanco County.

ROLLINS. John Quincy Adams Rollins was an early cattle rancher in an area lying to the south and west of the city of Boulder, in what is now Gilpin County. Sometime around 1861, he founded a mining camp he proudly called Rollinsville. This mining camp was unique in that saloons, gambling houses and dance halls were not allowed. Despite these burdensome limitations, Rollinsville survived and still exists as a town (population 181 in 2010) along Colorado Highway 119. To the west of Rollinsville is Rollins Pass, an 11,660-foot pass over the Continental Divide. The road over Rollins Pass, such as it was, was shut down by a rock collapse inside the Needle's Eye Tunnel in 1990. There has been a controversy ever since whether the road, in one form or another, should be reopened. So far, it has not been.

RUEDI. John Ruedi was a Swiss immigrant who, in the 1880s, found himself a nice little place to settle down and farm in the Fryingpan River Valley, in west-central Colorado, east of Basalt and not far from Aspen. This eventually led to the creation of a town in the area named Ruedi. Ruedi became something of a boomtown when the Colorado Midland Railway completed a rail line from Leadville, on the east, to Basalt, on the west, running right through the town. All of this became moot with the construction of Ruedi Reservoir as part of the Bureau of Reclamation's controversial Fryingpan-Arkansas Project, which takes water out of the Fryingpan River on the west side of the Continental Divide and sends it to the east side of the Continental Divide, into the Arkansas River. What was once the town of Ruedi now sits at the bottom of the reservoir.

SLOAN. Sloan's Lake, a 177-acre lake in west Denver, is named after a homesteader named Thomas F. Sloan who once owned the land where the lake is located. The formation of the lake seems to be a mystery since, according to one observer who departed the area in 1861 and returned in 1863, the lake wasn't there when he left but was there when he returned. Legend has it that Sloan, in the course of drilling a well for himself, tapped into an aquifer, resulting in a gusher that created the lake. The lake is now the centerpiece of a popular Denver urban park. The town of Edgewater borders the lake on its west side.

SPRINGFIELD. This name comes from Springfield, Missouri. The land for the town site for Springfield, Colorado, was purchased from a man from Springfield, Missouri; that was apparently enough to give the town its name. Springfield, Colorado, is in Baca County, in the far southeast corner of the state. It was first settled in the late 1880s, sits close to the panhandle of Oklahoma and shares that state's penchant for tornadoes. A category F4 tornado ravaged Springfield on May 18, 1977.

STERLING. This name comes from Sterling, Illinois, hometown of a railroad surveyor named David Leggett, who established a ranch in far northeast Colorado that evolved into the town of Sterling. Sterling, first settled around 1868, is the county seat for Logan County (which is indistinguishable from nearby western Nebraska). One of the last great battles of what became known as the Indian Wars—the Battle of Summit Springs—took place near Sterling in 1869. The Indians, from a branch of the Cheyenne tribe, were led by Chief Tall Bull. The United States Army was under the command of Colonel Eugene Carr, known affectionately as the "black-bearded Cossack." The army greatly prevailed in this battle, and Tall Bull was killed. William (aka Buffalo Bill) Cody later claimed he killed Tall Bull the day after the battle. What actually happened, however, is that Buffalo Bill killed another Indian who had taken and was riding Tall Bull's distinctive white horse after Tall Bull's death at the hands of Colonel Carr's soldiers during the battle.

SWINK. This name, given to a town along U.S. Highway 50 east of Pueblo and west of La Junta, and near Rocky Ford, comes from George Swink. George was a farmer in the area in the 1870s and is credited with turning this part of Colorado into a world-famous producer of cantaloupe and watermelon. When Swink told an acquaintance he missed the melons that grew in whatever part of the country he had come from, his acquaintance had his father (a one-time governor of Massachusetts) send out some cantaloupe and watermelon seeds, which were then given to Swink. The rest is history. Of far less importance than his cantaloupe and watermelon growing prowess, George Swink at one time served as a Colorado state senator.

TIMNATH. This name comes from the fourteenth chapter of the seventh book of the Old Testament, the book of Judges. As you probably already know, in the book of Judges, Timnath is the place where Samson goes to find a Philistine wife. The name made its way to Colorado in 1884 when a Presbyterian minister, Charles Taylor, gave the name to a town in north-central Colorado (Larimer County), to the south and east of Fort Collins. Reverend Taylor was the first postmaster for the town, which gave him naming rights. The town is still an agricultural hub, but development in the vicinity of Fort Collins to the north and west, and Windsor to the south and east, is encroaching on that way of life.

TRIMBLE. This name comes from a man named Frank Trimble, who discovered a hot spring on his property many years ago but doesn't seem to be remembered for anything else. The hot spring is now a tourist stop (including an Olympic-size swimming pool) along U.S. Highway 550 some nine miles north of Durango, in southwest Colorado. There's also Trimble Pass (12,874 feet), crossed by a hiking trail only, in the rugged San Juan Mountains to the north and east of Durango.

VILAS. This name comes from William F. Vilas, secretary of the interior from 1888 to 1889 under President Grover Cleveland. Before that, Vilas was the United States postmaster general. Although he was from Wisconsin and may never have set foot in Colorado, his name was given to a small town in the far southeast corner of the state (Baca County) founded in 1888. This naming may have been in furtherance of the goal of having a post office granted to the town. Back then, schmoozing politicians and bureaucrats by using their name was a common strategy employed by new towns wanting to obtain an official U.S. post office.

WALDEN. This name comes from Marcus Aurelius Walden, a local postmaster for a town in north-northwest Colorado founded in 1888 and originally (and appropriately) called Sagebrush. This town is the only incorporated municipality in Jackson County. It sits off the beaten path in a high mountain valley known as North Park and is a popular stopping place for Colorado hunters and fishermen.

WESTON. There are two Westons leaving their mark in Colorado. The unincorporated town of Weston ("town" may be an exaggeration these days) was named for a local blacksmith, S.A. "Bert" Weston, who convinced the U.S. Post Office to appoint him postmaster in 1892. This town sits near the New Mexico border along Colorado Highway 12, which is part of the Highway of Legends Scenic and Historic Byway connecting Walsenburg with Trinidad. In the late 1800s, the town epitomized the Wild West, with five saloons and a busy jail. It seems also to have been a favorite target for bank robbers. As for the second Weston, in west-central Colorado we have Weston Pass. This pass crosses over the Mosquito Range and connects Fairplay on the east with Leadville on the west. The pass, topping out at 11,921 feet, was named after A.S. Weston, who started ranching on the Leadville side of the pass in the 1860s and ended up as a Leadville lawyer with, apparently, a thriving practice during Leadville's mining boomtown days. (To muddy the waters a bit, there was also a Philo M. Weston, who ranched on the east side of the pass. But the better theory has the pass being named after A.S. Weston.) A county road, mostly unpaved, crosses over Weston Pass. Although you wouldn't want to take your Porsche Carrera on this road, a two-wheel-drive vehicle, driven carefully and with good shocks, is likely to survive the journey. This road was a toll road for a while in the second half of the nineteenth century, and back then it was known (optimistically) as the Road to Riches.

WILKERSON. Wilkerson Pass (9,507 feet) is fifty or so miles west of Colorado Springs on U.S. Highway 24, a major highway crossing the state from east to west (or west to east, depending on which way you're going). The pass sits at the east end of South Park and offers dramatic views of the vast expanse of South Park and several surrounding mountain ranges, including the

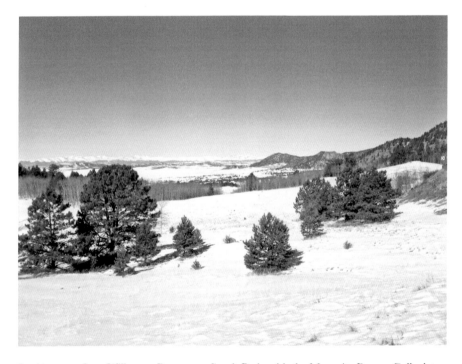

Looking west from Wilkerson Pass across South Park, with the Mosquito Range, Collegiate Range and Sangre de Cristo Range mountains in the background. *Photo by author.*

Mosquito Range, the Sangre de Cristo Range and the Collegiate Range, each of which contains many of Colorado's fourteeners. There's a rest area at the top of the pass with interpretive information placards, restrooms and a thriving population of boldly assertive chipmunks. The source of the name, however, is a mystery. The Colorado Department of Highways requested and received approval of the name from the United States Board on Geographic Names back in 1963, but the application contains no information about the source of the name—only a reference that it had appeared on a 1956 Park County highway map. The best theory I've come across so far is that an old ranching family named Wilkinson lived in the area, and somewhere along the way in the naming of the pass, Wilkinson got changed to Wilkerson. (There is no reason to believe the United States Post Office was responsible for this name mutation.)

XENIA. This name most likely comes from Xenia, Ohio, in the southwest part of that state and the county seat for Greene County, Ohio. However, how the name came to be given to a small, out-of-the-way town in east-central (Washington County) Colorado isn't known. Possibly it came from a homesick pioneer who, surrounded by the brown dusty sagebrush of eastern Colorado, missed the green grass of Ohio. Xenia, Ohio, got its name in the early 1800s at the suggestion of a minister familiar with the Greek language who said Xenia meant "hospitality" in that language. He thought this would be a good name for the Ohio community since he had been treated well upon his arrival there. In the Russian language, Xenia is a common name given to a woman. Xenia, Colorado, began, in 1883, as a construction campsite for the Burlington and Missouri River Railroad.

CHAPTER 8

GEOLOGY AND
GEOGRAPHY, FLORA
AND FAUNA

Colorado is geologically, geographically and biologically diverse. There are all manner of minerals to be found here (with the possible exception of diamonds, although there was actually a diamond rush in Colorado in 1872 in response to a gigantic—and profitable for the criminals—mine seeding fraud). There are plentiful sites throughout the state for the study of geologic periods, as well as the animals and plants that lived during those periods.

The eastern half of Colorado is high plains. The western half contains the mountains. The highest point in the state is Mount Elbert at 14,440 feet. The lowest point is in Yuma County at 3,315 feet. However, that low point is the highest low point of any state in the United States. San Juan County has the highest mean elevation of any county in the country at 11,240 feet, and twenty-three of the country's highest mean elevation counties are in Colorado.

Colorado has four main river systems, each moving water coming out of the mountains in a different direction—the Colorado River (west), the South Platte River (east), the Arkansas River (southeast) and the Rio Grande (south).

Colorado has only two natural lakes of any consequence: Grand Lake and Lake San Cristobal. However, the need to capture snowmelt for irrigation to support cities and agriculture has resulted in the construction of hundreds of dams and reservoirs, as well as complex (and controversial) trans-mountain water diversion projects.

Colorado's diverse geology and geography has produced plant and animal diversity as well. The state has everything from moose to Preble's

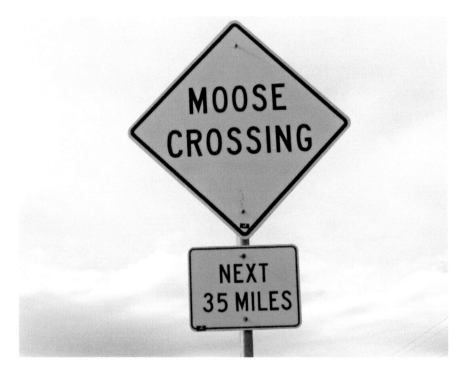

Share the road. *Photo by author.*

jumping mice and from cacti to watermelons. All of this diversity, as you might expect, has worked its way into the naming of Colorado places, going back to the earliest explorers and continuing today.

———◆———

BASALT. This name comes from a dark, hard and often glassy volcanic rock found in many locations in Colorado. (Although you probably already know this, basalt is primarily composed of plagioclase, augite and magnetite.) Because this stuff is plentiful where the Fryingpan River enters into the Roaring Fork River, a town at this location was eventually named Basalt. Previously, the town had been known as Aspen Junction and, before that, Fryingpan Junction.

BLACK CANYON. The Black Canyon of the Gunnison River, now a national park, got its name because parts of this very deep and rugged canyon receive only a small amount of sunlight on any given day. The

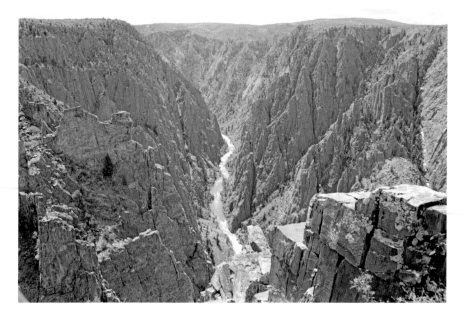

North rim, Black Canyon of the Gunnison River National Park. *Photo by author.*

national park includes twelve miles of the river in the deepest and most dramatic section of the canyon.

BOULDER. This name as used throughout Colorado comes from, well, boulders. Boulder County was one of the original seventeen counties making up the Colorado Territory when the territory was created in 1861. The county was named after Boulder City and Boulder Creek, both of which have lots of boulders. For the most part, Boulder County has retained its original dimensions, although some 27.5 square miles were carved off in 2001 and made a part of the City and County of Broomfield.

BOW MAR. This name comes from combining the names of two lakes—Bowles Lake and Marsten Lake—that are located in an area between Littleton on the east and Lakewood on the west. These lakes were, in turn, named after two pioneer farmers in the area, Joseph Bowles and John Marsten. The Bow Mar name was then given to a small (0.68-square-mile) town, 12 miles west of Denver, adjacent to the lakes. Bow Mar is partly in Jefferson County and partly in Arapahoe County and has managed to survive the development and annexation activity that has gone on all around it. Bow Mar consists of some three hundred one-acre upscale home sites and, among other things, prides itself on having a yacht club that regularly holds regattas on one of its namesake lakes.

BROOMFIELD. This name comes from a plant, broomcorn (for purists, *Sorghum vulgare technicum*). The plant is a grass that has stiff branching stalks, which can be used to make brooms and brushes. The city of Broomfield, located in an area where they grow this stuff, was incorporated in 1961. Back then, the city was entirely in Boulder County, but it grew and eventually oozed into three adjacent counties, creating a governmental nightmare. In 1998, the Colorado Constitution was amended to allow for the formation of the City and County of Broomfield, which finally got going as a single governmental unit in 2001. This is the newest and smallest of Colorado's sixty-four counties.

CAÑON. Cañon City, the county seat for Fremont County, got its name from the dramatic Arkansas River canyon to its west, now known as the Royal Gorge and previously known as the Grand Canyon of the Arkansas River. Cañon City was first settled in 1858, during the early days of the Colorado gold rush. Until 1994, its name was Canon City, without the little squiggly thing (called a "tilde") above the first *n*. In that year, however, the United States Board

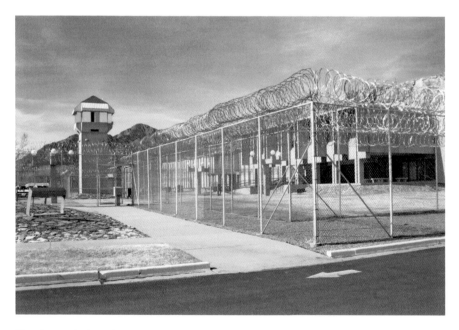

The Colorado State Penitentiary in Cañon City—a place you don't want to be, but a major source of employment in the area. *Photo by author.*

on Geographic names approved adding the squiggly thing. Cañon City's largest industry is prisons. There are thirteen such facilities in and around the city—nine state and four federal. It's a good idea to obey the speed limit in this area.

CASTLE. As you would expect, places are given the name "castle" because something there, or nearby, is "castellated," a term that means having turrets and battlements. Castle Peak meets this test. At 14,265 feet, this is Colorado's twelfth-highest mountain, the highest peak in the Elk Mountains (west-central Colorado), sits right on the line between Pitkin County and Gunnison County and is the highest point in both counties. The town of Castle Rock, between Denver and Colorado Springs, gets its name from a prominent castellated chunk of rock that sits atop a high butte on the east side of the I-25 corridor overlooking the city. Although formerly a manual operation, these days the American flag that sits on top of this rock is raised and lowered by a remotely operated electric motor. Castle Rock is the largest municipality in Colorado (population now exceeding fifty-five thousand) chartered as a town rather than a city.

CHALK. Chalk Creek is a twenty-seven-mile tributary of the Arkansas River with its headwaters along the Continental Divide in the Collegiate Peaks Range, between Mount Antero and Mount Princeton. The creek enters the Arkansas near the town of Nathrop (originally also named Chalk Creek). The creek gets its name from the white cliffs that are at the entrance to the Chalk Creek Valley and are clearly visible from U.S. Highway 285 to the south of Buena Vista and east of Mount Princeton. The white color comes from a mineral called kaolinite deposited by the hot springs in this area. Although you probably already knew this, kaolinite is the main ingredient in a fine clay compound called kaolin, used in the manufacture of ceramics, paper and textiles.

CLEAR CREEK. Clear Creek is a sixty-six-mile tributary of the South Platte River that begins in the mountains around Loveland Pass and the Eisenhower Tunnel and heads eastward. Because of a large number of medium-size round rocks in the river, Clear Creek was originally named Cannonball Creek by French hunters passing through the area in 1820. The creek, which isn't always clear, runs past the Coors brewery in Golden, Colorado, and no doubt contributes to the makeup of Colorado's most famous malt beverage. Clear Creek was a hotbed of early mining activity during the 1859 Colorado gold rush. Clear Creek County was one of Colorado's original seventeen counties, created in November 1861 shortly after Colorado became a territory. It is one of only two Colorado counties whose dimensions have not changed since first created. The other is Gilpin County. If (or rather when) you're stuck in a traffic jam on Interstate 70 in the vicinity of Idaho Springs or Georgetown, you'll be in Clear Creek County.

COLORADO SPRINGS. Colorado Springs is Colorado's second-most populous municipality, behind the City and County of Denver. However, the "springs" for which the city was named are not actually there—they are in Manitou Springs, a much smaller town to the west (and quite possibly the motel capital of the world). Colorado Springs formerly had a spring, in Monument Valley Park along Monument Creek. This spring was given the name Tahama, after a Sioux Indian chief and scout who traveled with Zebulon Pike while he was wandering around Colorado in the early 1800s. Sometime around 1926, a small pavilion was built at the site of the spring as part of a commemoration of Colorado's fiftieth anniversary as a state. Unfortunately, the pavilion took a hit when a flood tore through Monument Valley Park in 1935 and again when a second flood struck the area in 1965. This led to removal of the pavilion, and now only a small stone mound marks the site and caps the spring, leaving Colorado Springs without any actual spring. Colorado Springs sits at the foot of Pikes Peak and is the home of the United States Olympic Committee and the United States Air Force Academy. It is also blessed with one of the ranking natural wonders of the world, the Garden of the Gods, which the city maintains as a park, open free to the public.

DELTA. This name comes from a delta of land formed where the Gunnison and Uncompahgre Rivers come together. The name was given to a town at this location in the early 1880s. The town was originally called Uncompahgre, but it was later changed to Delta (probably because no one could correctly pronounce—let alone spell—Uncompahgre). The town had its beginnings way back in 1828 as a trading post called Fort Uncompahgre, used by early settlers and local iterations of the Ute Indian tribe. Those were apparently better times, when diplomacy and peaceful commerce prevailed over land grabs and warfare. The town of Delta, along U.S. Highway 50 in western Colorado, is the county seat of Delta County.

DINOSAUR. As you would expect, this name comes from those well-known and often large former inhabitants of the earth, whose fossil remains have been found in considerable abundance in far northwestern Colorado. The town of Dinosaur, in Moffat County, took this name in 1966 following the establishment

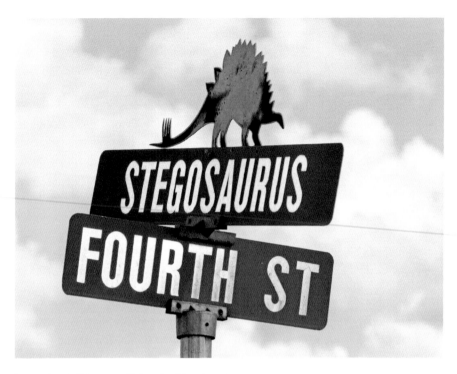

Street sign in Dinosaur, Colorado. *Photo by author.*

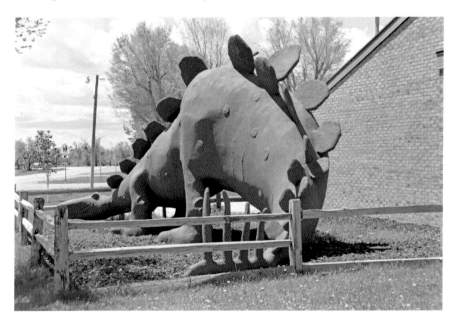

Dinosaur, Colorado Town Hall. *Photo by author.*

of nearby Dinosaur National Monument. Before that, the town was named Artesia, after a town in New Mexico and because of the presence of artesian wells in the area. Not only did the town change its name in an effort to cash in on the presence of the national monument as a major tourist draw, but it also changed the name of many of its streets. When visiting the town of Dinosaur, you will now find yourself on Brontosaurus Boulevard, Triceratops Terrace and Plateosaurus Place, among other dinosaur-inspired street names.

EDGEWATER. This name was given to a town immediately to the west of Denver because the town sits at the edge of Sloan's Lake. Sloan's Lake was formed when a homesteader named Thomas Sloan dug a well and, to his considerable surprise, hit a gusher of groundwater. Edgewater is a municipal island, surrounded by Lakewood on the south and west, Wheat Ridge on the north and Denver on the east. It was incorporated in 1904 and, as of the 2010 census, had some 5,100 residents.

ELEVEN MILE. This name comes from an eleven-mile-long canyon through which the South Platte River flows from South Park on its way to Denver and beyond. In addition to Eleven Mile Canyon, we now also have Eleven Mile Reservoir and Eleven Mile State Park, all in Park County. The South Platte River through the canyon is a popular fly fishing venue where, on occasion, the fishermen seem to outnumber the fish (and the fish are the smarter of the two).

FOUNTAIN. The town of Fountain, along Fountain Creek just south of Colorado Springs, took its name from the creek. The name of the creek, which has its headwaters up Ute Pass on the northeast side of Pikes Peak, came from French trappers and traders in the area who called it *Rivière de la Fontaine Qui Bouille*, the "River of the Fountain that Boils." The boiling part of this relates to the bubbling hot springs in the town of Manitou Springs, through which the creek flows (and occasionally floods). The town of Fountain was founded in 1859 as a railroad shipping terminal, serving the needs of farmers and ranchers in the area. A train accident there in 1888 resulted in a horrific explosion and fire that claimed several lives and left an unsolved mystery as to how a train parked on the tracks in Colorado Springs and loaded with blasting powder began coasting backward— southbound—in the path of a northbound train coming from Pueblo.

GRAND. Grand County and Grand Lake, in north-central Colorado, and Grand Junction, in west-central Colorado, took their names from the Grand River, the name originally given to the Colorado River. The river has its headwaters in Grand County. Grand County was formed on February 2 (now Groundhog Day) in 1874. The county lost some of its territory when Routt County was formed in 1877. Also, Grand County ended up in a nasty legal fight with neighboring Larimer County over land in a part of Colorado called North Park after valuable mineral deposits were discovered there. The case went all the way to the Colorado Supreme Court, where, in an 1886 decision, Larimer County was declared the winner. Grand Lake is the largest natural lake in Colorado and a beautiful place. Grand Junction got its name because this is where the Gunnison River empties into the Colorado River, formerly the Grand River. Grand Junction is the county seat for Mesa County and the most populous city in Colorado west of the Continental Divide.

GYPSUM. Gypsum is a soft sulfate mineral—for purists, calcium sulfate dihydrate, aka $CaSO_4(H_2O)_2$—that is found in abundance in various places in Colorado. It is used as a fertilizer and in the manufacture of some forms of plaster, including plaster of Paris (so named because the stuff was once extensively mined in the Montmartre district of Paris). You may also have encountered gypsum as the primary ingredient in blackboard chalk. Because of large deposits in the area, this mineral gave its name to a town in west-central Colorado (Eagle County) along Interstate 70, with a current population of something like 6,500. There is additionally a 6,100-foot pass in western Colorado, along Colorado Highway 141, known as Gypsum Gap, first named by Spanish explorers in 1776.

HOLY CROSS. This name, of course, comes from Christian symbolism. Early explorers of the wilds of Colorado (and who had to be deeply religious or they never would have gone on these trips) gave Christian names to all kinds of things. Mount of the Holy Cross, in the Sawatch Range in central Colorado, ranks, at

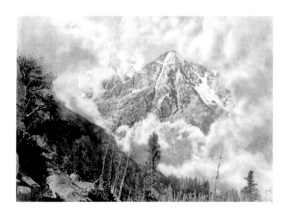

Mount of the Holy Cross—next to Pikes Peak, perhaps Colorado's most famous mountain. *William Henry Jackson, Library of Congress, ID PPMSCA 17835.*

14,005 feet, fifty-first on the list of Colorado's fifty-three 14,000-foot peaks. The mountain got its name, first officially reported in 1869, because of a snow field on its northeast face that, with some imagination, resembles a gigantic cross. William H. Jackson, a pioneering photographer with the U.S. Government Hayden Survey, was, in 1873, finally able to get close enough to the mountain to photograph its namesake snow field. Jackson took his now famous photograph from nearby Notch Mountain.

Horsetooth. This name comes from a prominent rock formation some seven miles west of Fort Collins that looks like a tooth from a horse. The rock formation is at the summit of a small (7,259-foot) mountain known, not surprisingly, as Horsetooth Mountain. Horsetooth Reservoir, also near Fort Collins and a part of the Colorado–Big Thompson trans-mountain water diversion project, additionally derives its name from this rock formation.

Hot Sulphur Springs. This town, founded in 1860 along the Colorado River and now along U.S. Highway 40, got its name because of the hot springs in the area. In 1863, William Byers, the owner of the *Rocky Mountain News*, purchased the town site from a Sioux Indian woman whose title to the land was not exactly squeaky clean, especially since this land had been given to the Ute Indians as part of one of the many treaties the United States entered into with the Utes and then largely ignored. The Utes challenged Byers's title to the land in a legal proceeding but lost. Byers was later a leader in a "the Utes must go" campaign, assisted in that effort by, among others, territorial governors William Gilpin and John Evans. The town of Hot Sulphur Springs celebrates Halloween on October 30 rather than October 31. That's because in the old days, the last day of the month was payday, which regularly generated gunfights and made the town unsafe for children.

Lake. This name was given to one of Colorado's original seventeen counties in 1861 in recognition of Twin Lakes—two back-to-back lakes within the county's borders (and home to some really big lake trout). Lake County originally covered much more land than it does today. It lost land to adjacent counties in 1866, 1874, 1876, 1877 and 1879. Lake County was renamed Carbonate County for two days in February 1879. But then Chaffee County was formed, and the Lake County name was reinstated. Colorado's highest mountain, Mount Elbert, is in Lake County. Mount Elbert rises to 14,440 feet (or, if you're a metric-thinking person, 4,401.2 meters). The most northerly part of the Arkansas River Headwaters Recreational Area is in Lake County, as is the city of Leadville.

LARKSPUR. This name comes from a flower that is common in the vicinity of the town of Larkspur. The flower (*Delphinium geyeri*) is nice to look at but apparently poisonous to livestock. The town of Larkspur, in Douglas County north of Colorado Springs and south of Castle Rock, was first established in the 1860s as a Denver and Rio Grande railway station.

LIZARD HEAD. We have a Lizard Head Peak (13,133 feet) and a Lizard Head Pass (10,222 feet), both in southwest Colorado and both named after a very distinct mountain summit that, among other things, looks like a gigantic lizard poking its head up out of the ground to have a look around. Colorado Highway 145 crosses over the pass and is paved.

MARBLE. The town of Marble got its name from the marble rock formations in the area, located principally in what became known as the Yule quarry. The marble there is of high quality, has been mined for more than one hundred years and has been installed in famous buildings throughout the world, including the Lincoln Monument and the Tomb of the Unknowns. The town is in Gunnison County, along the Crystal River, and in recent years has become a favorite Colorado tourist hangout.

MAROON. This name comes from the color. The U.S. Government Hayden Survey of 1874 gave the name Maroon Mountain to what is now officially known as Maroon Peak. Maroon Peak, near Aspen, is in the Elk Range and, at 14,156 feet, ranks as Colorado's twenty-fourth-highest mountain. There are two summits here in proximity, connected by a saddle, and because of their bell-shaped configuration, locals started calling them collectively the Maroon Bells, a name that stuck. Although both Maroon Bells summits are over 14,000 feet, only the south summit—Maroon Peak—makes it onto the list of Colorado's fourteeners. North Maroon Peak doesn't qualify because of the "prominence rule," which says that a summit must rise at least 300 feet above the saddle connecting it to another, higher, 14,000-foot summit in order to be given separate recognition as a fourteener. In addition to North Maroon Peak, there are four other summits in Colorado over 14,000 feet having separate names but that fail the prominence test and therefore don't make it onto the official list of fourteeners. These are Mount Cameron (connected to Mount Lincoln), El Diente (connected to Mount Wilson), Conundrum Peak (connected to Castle Peak) and North Eolus (connected to Mount Eolus).

MASSIVE. Mount Massive, at 14,421 feet, is Colorado's second-highest mountain. It got its name because it is indeed massive. It has five summits above 14,000 feet and a summit ridge that stretches more than three miles. This results in the largest surface area above 14,000 feet of any mountain in the forty-eight contiguous states, narrowly beating out Mount Rainier for this honor. Mount Massive was first climbed in 1873 by Henry Gannet, a member of the Hayden Survey party.

MERINO. This name comes from a breed of sheep, prized for centuries for its soft wool. The name was given to a small town in far northeast Colorado (Logan County) where these critters once grazed in abundance. The town was first established in 1874 and was at that time known as Buffalo. The name was changed to Merino in 1882 when the

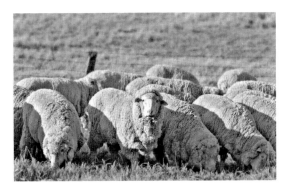

Merino sheep—the inspiration for the naming of a town in far northeast Colorado originally called Buffalo. *Merino fir0002, flagstaffoto.com.au.*

Union Pacific Railroad constructed a spur through the area. By then, the railroaders had probably had their fill of buffalo, and no doubt the buffalo population had already been decimated by hunters.

MESA. The name "mesa," like "boulder," shows up often in Colorado because the state has lots of them. A mesa is a flat-topped elevation with one or more cliff-like sides. Mesa County, a carve-out from Gunnison County in west-central Colorado, was named after these things in 1883. If you're ever in the area, you'll know why.

MONUMENT. This name comes from rock formations, one of which lies to the west of the town of Monument in northern El Paso County. This town sits at the foot of Monument Hill, a 7,352-foot-high point along Interstate 25 notorious for black ice, blizzards, hail, high winds and other conditions that regularly snare unsuspecting motorists. Another noteworthy name-inspiring rock formation is a natural stone obelisk that sticks up out of Monument Lake, a reservoir in Las Animas County.

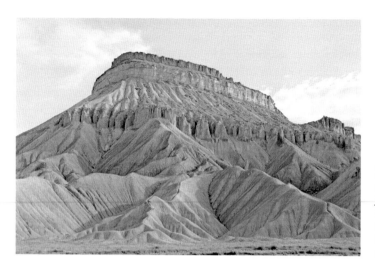

Palisades along I-70, just to the west of the town of Palisade, Colorado.
Photo by author.

PALISADE. A "palisade" is a line of steep, lofty cliffs. Such an area exists in Mesa County, some fifteen miles east of Grand Junction, and this was the source of the name for a town at that location, established in 1895. Palisade proved to be a highly productive area for fruit orchards (and, later, vineyards), causing it to become the self-proclaimed "Peach Capital of Colorado." Among other accomplishments, Palisade, as early as 1910, had a women's baseball team, although it's not clear where this team found competition.

PAONIA. Sometime around 1880, a pioneer rancher named Samuel Wade started a town in what is now Delta County, Colorado. Wade applied for a post office for this community and submitted the name Paeonia, which is Latin for the genus that includes the peony plant, specimens of which Wade had brought with him to Colorado from wherever he came from. Although Wade seems to have been well schooled in Latin botanical names, the United States Post Office was not, and it changed the name to Paonia. In addition to the town of Paonia, we have Paonia State Park, which lies to the east of the town, in Gunnison County. Highlights of the park include water recreation at Paonia Reservoir and—you don't find this just anywhere—fossilized palm fronds.

PARACHUTE. In Colorado, we have Parachute Creek, a tributary of the Colorado River, and the town of Parachute, located along the creek in Garfield County not far from the Interstate 70 corridor in west-central Colorado. At some point in the early 1900s, the town changed its name from

Parachute to Grand Valley, but in 1980, it brought back the original name. So, where did the "parachute" name come from in the first place? Well, this name shows up as the name of a creek on a map produced by the Hayden Survey—meaning in the early 1870s—and there are several theories about how the name came to be given to the creek. Most of these relate to the shape of the creek, especially when viewed from a high-up vista. One theory, however, has it that a long-ago hunter, looking down on the creek from the cliffs above it, said something like, "Wow, we're going to need a parachute to get down there." What you may not know—I certainly didn't—is that the idea of a parachute goes back a long way. There is a famous drawing of such a device by Leonardo da Vinci circa 1485. And a Frenchman, Louis-Sébastien Lenormand, made the first recorded descent using a parachute (and living to tell about it) in 1783. Lenormand, apparently the Evel Knievel of his day, is also credited with coming up with the name "parachute."

PARK. Park is, of course, a term with many meanings. One of those meanings is a parcel of royal land set aside for hunting. Colorado (officially, at least) has none of these. Another meaning of "park" is a flat, high-altitude basin surrounded by mountains. Colorado has three of these, cleverly named South Park, North Park and Middle Park. South Park, at the geographic center of Colorado, is the largest, measuring approximately one thousand square miles, or 640,000 acres. (For the technically inclined, South Park is further described by geologists as "a wide faulted syncline of sedimentary rocks.") North Park lies in north-central Colorado and is home to parts of the North Platte River, known to trout fishermen everywhere as a place to catch—or try to catch—really big fish. Middle Park, the smallest of the three mountain parks, is also in north-central Colorado, just to the south of North Park. Middle Park, on the west side of the Front Range, includes Grand Lake and other parts of the headwaters of the Colorado River. Park County received its name from South Park. It was formed in 1861 as one of the original seventeen counties making up the Colorado Territory. Presumably, the animated sitcom *South Park* also derived its name from this part of Colorado.

POWDERHORN. This name comes from a device made from an animal horn with a plug on one end used to store gunpowder. Powderhorns were popular back in the days of muzzle-loading rifles and pistols, before the invention of bullets. How the name came to be associated with a valley and a town in Gunnison County, as well as a few high mountain lakes and a federal wilderness area, is not precisely known. Theories include: (1) a pioneer once found a powderhorn in the area a long time ago; (2) the valley formed by Cebolla Creek has the shape of a cow's horn; and (3) a prominent long ridge starting at the Continental Divide and gradually descending in an easterly direction toward the Cebolla Creek valley has the shape of a cow's horn. Take your pick. The small town of Powderhorn, between Blue Mesa Reservoir on the north and Lake City on the south, was originally a health resort called White Earth.

PYRAMID. This name, of course, comes from the ancient pyramids of Egypt and their distinctive shape. Following in that tradition, one of Colorado's fourteeners is named Pyramid Peak because, with a little imagination, its summit resembles a pyramid. Pyramid Peak, which at 14,018 feet ranks forty-seventh on the list of the fifty-three Colorado mountains over 14,000 feet, was originally named Black Pyramid Peak by the Hayden Survey in 1874. Apparently, that sounded too sinister, and the name was later changed to just Pyramid Peak. Pyramid Peak is in the Elk Mountain Range, in west-central Colorado, not far from Aspen. Lest you be confused about this, there are also mountains named Pyramid Peak in California, Montana, Washington, Idaho and Antarctica.

RABBIT EARS. This name comes from a distinctive body part of a commonly seen animal in the family *Laporidae*. In Colorado, the name is associated with a mountain top, Rabbit Ears Peak, easily seen along U.S. Highway 40 when you're heading north out of Kremmling on your way to Steamboat Springs. This drive also takes you over Rabbit Ears Pass, which tops out at 9,426 feet and is famous for big snowfalls, high winds, road closures and mountain rescues. There is additionally an Old Rabbit Ears Pass, traversed by Grand County Road 199. Old Rabbit Ears Pass, at 9,573 feet, is slightly higher than the current Rabbit Ears Pass and is capable of producing even worse winter weather.

ROAN. This name is believed to come from a color scheme popular with certain makes and models of horses, involving a gray, brown or chestnut primary color speckled with white. The rugged fifty-four-thousand-acre Roan Plateau in west-central Colorado, north and west of the town of Rifle, was for many years ground zero for a heated debate between hunters, fishermen and environmentalists on the one hand and oil and gas development interests on the other hand. (The area was once known as the Naval Oil Shale Reserve.) A peace treaty of sorts was achieved in 2014 by reason of an agreement that terminated some of the mining leases the federal government had previously granted in the area.

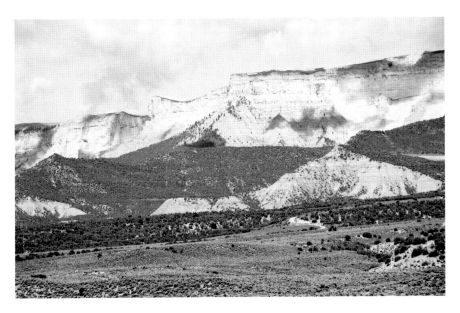

Southeast flank of the Roan Plateau, just to the west of Rifle, Colorado. *Photo by author.*

SHRINE. Shrine Pass is a mountain pass that connects I-70 on the east, as it crosses over Vail Pass, with the town of Red Cliff on the west. It got its name because people hoping for a meaningful religious experience would climb to the summit to gaze upon the Mount of the Holy Cross. (This worked best on a clear day.) The road over Shrine Pass is part paved and part gravel and is 11.2 miles in length. The road purports to be drivable in the summer with a regular passenger vehicle, but I wouldn't count on that. It is better used for a winter cross-country ski trip, where you leave a second vehicle at one end or the other, stocked with ample quantities of your favorite malt beverage to celebrate the end of your trip. The summit elevation is 11,094 feet.

SILT. This name comes from a type of dirt that consists of particles somewhere between clay and sand in size. The name Silt was given to a town in west-central Colorado (Garfield County) along the Colorado River, and now along I-70, by the Denver and Rio Grande Western Railroad because there was lots of this stuff present at the town site. The town, not established until 1908, was originally called Ferguson, but that name didn't catch on with the locals. The community has a catchy motto: "Silt Happens."

SLUMGULLION. We can thank a large landslide in the San Juan Mountains for this name. The landslide began seven hundred years ago, had a reawakening

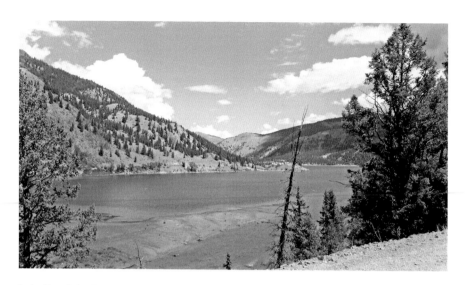

Lake San Cristobal, near Lake City. This is Colorado's second-largest natural lake, formed when the Slumgullion Earthflow created a dam across the Lake Fork of the Gunnison River. *Wikimedia Commons.*

three hundred years ago and is still active today. The landslide area has a yellowish color that reminded earlier settlers of slumgullion stew, a watery meat-and-potatoes stew well known in Ireland and Scotland. (Another explanation has it that the term "slumgullion" refers to what was left after a whale has been butchered. I prefer the stew theory.) You can plainly see the landslide—technically known as the Slumgullion Earthflow—while driving north on Colorado Highway 149 from Creede to Lake City over Slumgullion Pass. The summit elevation of Slumgullion Pass is 11,530 feet, placing it eighth on the list of Colorado passes with a paved road—assuming you don't count the high point along Trail Ridge Road (too flat to be a pass) or Cottonwood Pass (only served by a paved road on the east side). The Slumgullion Earthflow created a natural dam across the Lake Fork of the Gunnison River, resulting in the formation of Lake San Cristobal, Colorado's second-largest natural lake.

SPIKEBUCK. This name comes from the anatomy of a young male deer. The little stubs that first appear on these critters when it's time to grow antlers and go looking for female deer are called spikebucks. One of the recreation sites and whitewater rafting landmarks along the Arkansas River in Bighorn Sheep Canyon, which is located between Salida and the Royal Gorge, is named Spikebuck. It's a great place to stop for a picnic lunch (and a bathroom break). In my experience, however, it's not a great place for catching trout. They seem to know you're there, and they ignore you.

STEAMBOAT. Steamboat Springs, now a world-famous ski resort in Routt County, got its name from one of the hot springs in the area that made a loud chugging sound similar to a steamboat. Unfortunately, this spring was destroyed during the construction of a railroad line in the early 1900s, so it is no more. An adventurous pioneer named James Harvey Crawford is credited with founding the town of Steamboat Springs. He first came to the area in 1874. The town gained momentum after the Ute Indians, who had lived and hunted in this part of Colorado for centuries, were marched off to a reservation following the 1879 Meeker Massacre. Steamboat Springs is the county seat for Routt County.

SUMMIT. Summit County in central Colorado was, of course, given its name because in this part of the state, there are mountains all over the place. Summit County is now home to the Arapahoe Basin, Breckenridge, Copper Mountain and Keystone ski areas. The county was formed in 1861 as one of the original seventeen counties making up the Colorado Territory. Various county boundary shuffles after that have caused parts of Summit County to become parts of Grand, Routt, Moffat, Garfield, Rio Blanco and Eagle Counties.

SUNSHINE. This name deserves mention because of Sunshine Peak. Sunshine Peak, in the San Juan Range in southwest Colorado, holds down last place (fifty-third) on the list of Colorado's 14,000-foot mountains. At 14,001 feet, Sunshine Peak just barely makes the cut. The mountain was climbed by members of the U.S. Government Hayden Survey in 1874. They, however, referred to the mountain on their maps simply as "Station 12," a triangulation reference point. The mountain wasn't officially named Sunshine Peak until 1904. Prior to that, it had been unofficially known as Niagra Peak and Sherman Mountain.

SYLVAN. This is a word that, as an adjective, means something like "relating to a forest." As a noun, a "sylvan" is someone who lives in or frequently visits the woods. So, if you wanted to demonstrate your in-depth knowledge of the English language, you could call some of your acquaintances who go camping a lot "sylvans" and see what kind of reaction you get. Colorado has used this word as the name for a state park—Sylvan Lake State Park. The park is in Eagle County, ten miles south of the town of Eagle. It is 1,548 acres in size, is surrounded by White River National Forest and has a forty-two-acre lake and no cellphone service.

Trail Ridge. This name, logically enough, refers to a ridge over which a trail was established long ago by various Indian tribes as a way to get across the mountains in what is now Rocky Mountain National Park. The Arapahoe Indians called this trail the "dog trail," although no one seems to know why. A road, Trail Ridge Road, now exists along Trail Ridge. Construction of the road, which took place between 1929 and 1938, was controversial due to its intrusion into pristine natural terrain, but the National Park Service went ahead anyway and did its best to mitigate the environmental and aesthetic impact of the road. Trail Ridge Road is the highest continuously paved road in the United States. It rises to 12,183 feet. Along the way, it crosses over three passes—Milner (10,758 feet), Fall River (11,796 feet) and Iceberg (11,827 feet). Because the road's high point is largely flat and therefore not considered a pass, Independence Pass, at 12,095 feet, gets to claim the title as Colorado's highest pass with a fully paved road. (Cottonwood Pass is higher than Independence Pass at 12,126 feet, but it only has a paved road on the east side. The road is gravel from the summit going west.)

Willow. This name comes from the abundant shrub-like plant that lines the banks of streams and rivers in Colorado, to the regular dismay of fly fishermen. I mention it only because "willow" takes top prize in Colorado as a name for a stream. One source I found said there are seventy-two Willow Creeks in this state. (By comparison, there are only forty-nine Bear Creeks, forty-nine Beaver Creeks and forty-eight Dry Creeks.)

Yellow Jacket. Although there might have been an old Indian named Yellow Jacket, this name most likely came from the insect (for entomologists, *Vespula maculinfrons*). Yellow Jacket Canyon, in far southwestern Colorado (Montezuma County) right at the Utah border, is plastered with their nests. The Yellow Jacket name, after it was given to the canyon, led to the naming of a small unincorporated community in the same area (worthy, but just barely, of a post office and a zip code). You'll find this community along rural Colorado Highway 491. There is also a Yellowjacket Pass (7,783 feet) along Colorado Highway 160 between Bayfield on the west and Pagosa Springs on the east. To confuse things a bit, there is another Yellow Jacket Pass (this time again spelled with "Yellow" and "Jacket" as separate words) in Routt County, south and west of Steamboat Springs and just to the north of Stagecoach Reservoir. This pass, traversed by a gravel road—County Road 114—tops out at 7,428 feet.

CHAPTER 9

THE MISFITS

There are numerous names appearing in this book that could have been included in more than one category. For example, many of the Spanish empire–inspired names also describe some aspect of Colorado's geology, geography, flora or fauna. There are a few names, however, that didn't seem to fit into any of the categories I created for purposes of organizing this material. These are the misfits.

———•———

ARKANSAS. The Arkansas River is a major Colorado and U.S. waterway, having its headwaters around Leadville, flowing south to Salida and then east/southeast clear across the state. After leaving Colorado, the river passes through Kansas and Oklahoma and into the state of Arkansas, where it empties into the Mississippi River. The total length of the river is 1,469 miles, making it the sixth-longest river in the United States. The river is now a Gold Medal fishing wonderland from its headwaters near Leadville to just west of the Royal Gorge and supports a major whitewater rafting industry from Buena Vista down to Cañon City. As for the name, well, the part of the river in Colorado had multiple names going all the way back to the days of the Spanish conquistadors in the 1500s, and it finally took an act of the Colorado legislature in 1881 to fix the name, together with an official pronunciation: *ar*-can-saw. (The river is still called ar-*kansas* by people

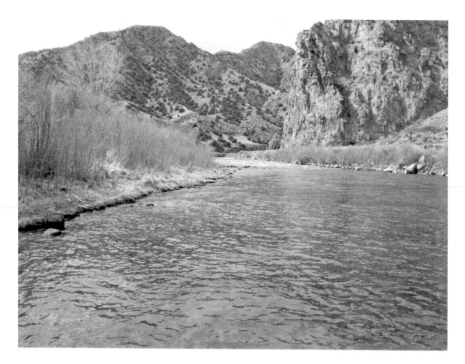

Arkansas River, just west of Cañon City. There are big trout in here, but they seem to be smarter than the average fisherman. *Photo by author.*

living in eastern Colorado and elsewhere.) Ultimately, the name seems to be a derivation of a word from an Indian language that had worked its way, in one mutated form or another, into the vocabulary of French explorers by the time they started wandering around Colorado in the 1600s. As an unrelated bit of trivia, the state of Arkansas came into being in 1836 as the country's twenty-fifth state.

BARKER. Barker Reservoir, near Nederland, is part of the water system serving the city of Boulder. The reservoir is named after Hannah Barker, who owned the land on which the reservoir was built. She refused to sell the land, resulting in a government condemnation action. Despite Hannah's decision to stand in the way of progress, the reservoir, and the dam that forms it, ended up carrying her name.

BISHOP. The Bishop I have in mind here is Jim Bishop, a resident of Pueblo who has spent almost half a century building a structure unlike anything else in the world, known as Bishop's Castle (or possibly Bishop's Folly). This

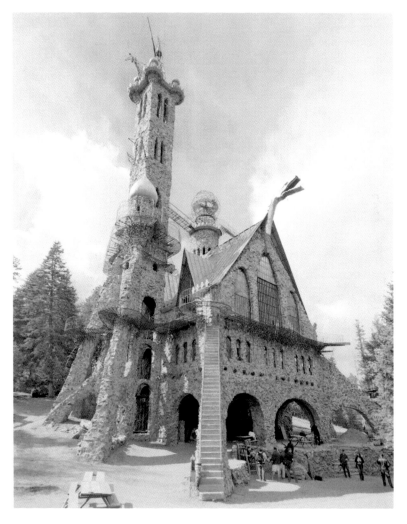

Bishop's Castle. You have to see it to believe it—and you may still not believe it.
Hustvedt, Wikimedia Commons.

project started out in 1969 as a vacation cabin, but it soon morphed into a stone and iron skeleton 160 feet tall located on 2.5 acres of land surrounded on three sides by San Isabel National Forest. It sits along Colorado Highway 165 (aka the Frontier Pathways Scenic and Historic Highway), not far from Rye, Colorado. Anyone willing to agree to Bishop's terms—that is, a complete release of liability—can visit his castle. Bishop's Castle has been an irritant to the U.S. Forest Service and various state and county agencies for decades and is a regular source of traffic snarls along Colorado Highway

165. However, its ability to bring tourist income to the area has seemingly resulted in a circumstance of governmental tolerance. Bishop's Castle is a work in progress—it is not complete and never will be. As of this writing, Jim Bishop is seriously ill and is having difficulty continuing with his project, and there are no successors standing in line to take his place.

CANNIBAL. This name shows up often in Colorado thanks to Alfred (aka Alferd) Packer, who allegedly killed and ate five of his companions during the harsh winter of 1874. Packer denied the killing but admitted the eating. This event took place near Lake City, in Hinsdale County. The Cannibal Plateau sits at the border of Hinsdale and Gunnison Counties, east and north a bit from Lake City and adjacent to the Powderhorn Wilderness Area. The Alferd Packer Restaurant and Grill can be found on the campus of the University of Colorado in Boulder, where humor sometimes takes a strange bent. The Packer Saloon & Cannibal Grill in Lake City helps to preserve the memory of Colorado's most famous cannibal.

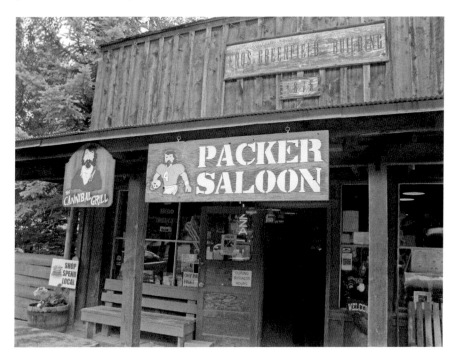

The Packer Saloon and Cannibal Grill in Lake City, Colorado. Alfred (aka Alferd) Packer, Colorado's most famous cannibal, was also the inspiration for the naming of one of the dining facilities on the University of Colorado campus in Boulder: the Alferd Packer Restaurant and Grill. *Ed Sealover.*

EOLUS. This name, with a slight change in spelling, comes from Greek mythology. According to Homer's *Odyssey*, Aeolus was the god of the winds. Aeolus tried to help Odysseus (aka Ulysses) in his quest to sail back to Ithaca by giving him a favorable west wind and a bag (a wind bag?) in which all the unfavorable winds had been sealed up and trapped. But some of Odysseus's nosey companions opened the bag to see what was in it and let all the unfavorable winds escape. This made Aeolus mad, and for Odysseus, things went downhill from there. Mount Eolus, in the Needle Mountains of southwest Colorado, is, at 14,083 feet, Colorado's thirty-second-highest peak. Climbers often get a lift into and out of the Needle Mountains area via the narrow-gauge train that runs between Durango and Silverton.

FRASER. The town of Fraser was named after the Fraser River, which has its headwaters on the north side of Berthoud Pass and then flows north/northwest some thirty-two miles to its confluence with the Colorado River, passing through Winter Park and Fraser along the way. But how the river got its name is not known. The name Fraser started showing up on maps in the late 1860s. Prior to that, in 1861, explorer Edward L. Berthoud had named it Moses Creek, after one of his assistants. But that name apparently didn't catch on with the locals. The town of Fraser was originally named Eastom, after George Eastom, who first laid out the town site. That name apparently also didn't catch on with the locals, so the name of the town was changed to the name of the river.

LADDER. A creek with its headwaters in far east-central Colorado (Cheyenne County) is named Ladder Creek. The creek flows some 230 miles eastward to a confluence with the Smokey Hill River in Logan County, Kansas. The name was given to the creek by a survey party that found an old ladder imbedded in dirt and grass by the side of the creek. This created a mystery for the survey party since there was no apparent use for a ladder in this location. The creek is known locally as Beaver Creek, along with forty-eight other creeks in Colorado having that name.

NO NAME. No Name is a small unincorporated community east of Glenwood Springs. Travelers along Interstate 70 as it passes through scenic Glenwood Canyon will see an exit sign (Exit 119) for the community. Also, two tunnels that are a part of this complex and hugely expensive section of the highway are known as the No Name Tunnels. Before the No Name name was given to the town (what there is of it), there was already a No Name Creek and a No Name Canyon, and the town sits between the two. The Colorado Department of Transportation once tried to give the town a right and proper name, but the locals, having become fond of the No Name name, protested. So, the No Name name has remained.

SNEFFELS. Here we have something of a mystery. Mount Sneffels, in the San Juan Range in southwestern Colorado, at 14,150 feet, holds position number twenty-seven on the list of Colorado's highest mountains. However, there are at least three theories as to where this name came from. One theory ties the name to a volcano in Iceland, Snaefell, featured in Jules Verne's 1864 novel *A Journey to the Center of the Earth*. In the novel, Mount Snaefell rose above the great hole in the surface of Earth by which the center of the Earth was to be reached. A second theory, much less dramatic, ties the name to someone named Sneffels who was associated with the U.S. Government Hayden Survey, four members of which (none named Sneffels) made the first recorded ascent of the peak in 1874. The third theory is that the name derived from "sniffles" because the miners in the area in the 1870s kept catching colds and also weren't much good at spelling.

The Regulation of Place Names in Today's World

Let's say you're on a multi-day backpacking trip in a remote area high in the San Juan Mountains and you come upon a small mountain lake—a tarn—that on all of the maps you have and your GPS system has no name. You decide you'd like to name this lake after your faithful dog, Roscoe, who has accompanied you on this trip and has been diligently protecting you from malevolent acts of wildlife (marmots, chipmunks, gray jays). Can you do this? The answer is: you can try, but your odds of success are roughly the same as winning the lottery. Here's why.

When remote areas of the western United States were being settled in the 1800s, the naming of geographic places was largely unregulated and resulted in chaos, with much duplication and poor recordkeeping. To address this problem, President Benjamin Harrison, on September 4, 1890, signed an executive order creating the United States Board on Geographic Names, whose mission it was to establish and maintain uniform geographic name usage throughout the federal government. This agency, a part of the United States Geological Survey within the Department of the Interior, continues to exist today, and its activities over the past 116 years have greatly expanded and have been greatly enhanced by technology. By way of example, there is now in place a comprehensive searchable database known as the Geographic Names Information System and a National Map. (This is fascinating. You can check it out at http://nationalmap.gov.)

If you want to propose a name for an unnamed geographic place, you can do so using an application provided by the board. (Go to http://geonames. usgs.gov to get the application.) In completing the application, however, you will need to adhere to a set of rules contained in a fifty-six-page document called "Principles, Policies & Procedures: Domestic Geographic Names." A few of the simpler rules to be found here are: you cannot name a place after a living person or after a dead person who has not been dead at least five years. (I found nothing about dogs, living or dead.)

In processing name applications, the board seeks to meet the needs of the multiple federal agencies making up its membership. This includes not only the Department of the Interior and the U.S. Geological Survey but also the Department of Defense, the National Geospatial-Intelligence Agency, the Central Intelligence Agency, the Department of Homeland Security, the U.S. Postal Service, the Government Publishing Office, the Department of State and the Library of Congress. As you can imagine, the bar for obtaining name approval is high.

Colorado, as do most other states, also has an agency with authority over geographic names. Colorado's agency, in keeping with the name of the federal agency, is called the Colorado Board on Geographic Names (http://colorado.gov/pacific/archives/cbgn). It seeks to cooperate with, and support the mission of, the national board, but it also has its own rules and policies.

The naming of roads, streets and highways is governed by other, often local, agencies and rules. Maybe Roscoe would have a better chance there.

INDEX

About the Author

J im Flynn grew up in Omaha, Nebraska; attended Dartmouth College on a National Merit Scholarship, majoring in French; and went on to earn a law degree from Stanford Law School. In between the start and finish of law school, Jim served as an officer in the United States Navy, assigned to a branch of the navy that specialized in electronic espionage and secure communications, 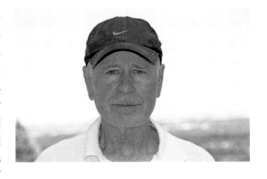 where he learned Mandarin Chinese. Jim practiced law in Colorado Springs for forty years, representing banks and other clients in the financial services industry and litigating commercial disputes. Jim lives in Colorado Springs with his wife, Anne Marie, and dogs Winston, a Golden retriever, and Abby, a not-sure-what. Jim has previously written three lawyer-related novels—*Overdraft*, about a cyber attack on the U.S. banking system; *Where There's No Will*, about a multimillion-dollar will contest in rural Gunnison County, Colorado, resulting from a missing will; and *Fraudulent Transfers*, about a counterfeit cashier's check fraud and a related money-laundering enterprise. He has also for many years written a weekly column for Colorado Springs' daily paper, the *Gazette*, called "Money & the Law." Whenever he can, Jim stalks trout in the rivers and lakes of Colorado, although the fish rarely feel threatened.